NOW IT CAN BE TOLD

Tales of the OSS

Marvin R. Edwards

with

Susan D. Brandenburg

Copyright © 2017

All rights reserved, including the right of
reproduction in whole or in part in any form.

ISBN: 978-0-9973135-6-7

This book was published in the U.S.A. by Susan the Scribe, Inc.
www.susanthescribe.vpweb.com

Layout and Design:
Philip Barnes
Riverducks Design
riverducksdesign@gmail.com

Cover Story
**The map on the cover of this book is Hitler's blueprint for a German air-strike of the English coastline by the Luftwaffe – an attack that never happened due to the unexpected strength and resistance of the Royal Air Force. I found this map being used as a tablecloth at Tempelhof Airport in 1946 and was told by the waiter that there were others in the basement.
As a navigator and a historian, I recognized the significance of these maps, which are now rare and valuable.**

**In my photo on the back cover, I am displaying
four map folios of Hitler's invasion plan
~ MRE – 2017.**

FOREWORD

The Office of Strategic Services (OSS) was the revolutionary World War II predecessor to the CIA and the US Special Operations Command. It played a decisive role in America's victory in World War II. It was founded and led by General William J. Donovan, a Medal of Honor recipient and one of the most remarkable people in our nation's history. OSS recruited some of America's most brilliant citizens. An ideal OSS candidate was described as a "Harvard Ph.D. who could handle himself in a bar fight." This includes Marvin Edwards who participated in some of the most secret and important missions of World War II. Edwards recounts his heroic service in the OSS with modesty that is a common characteristic for those who served at the "tip of the spear."

Reading his memoir, it becomes readily apparent why Edwards and the OSS were a perfect match. His interest in world affairs began at a young age. He predicted the coming world war with Germany in 1937. Recruited by the OSS, he was assigned to the 801st/492nd Bomb Group – the "Carpetbaggers" – that flew specially equipped B-24s on low-altitude, single-plane missions to deliver supplies and OSS personnel to support resistance movements in Nazi-occupied Europe. Edwards also flew in one of the most technically advanced aircraft built during the war: the legendary Mosquito, a Rolls-Royce powered aircraft that flew as high as 40,000 feet. It was used by the OSS in conjunction with an innovative communications device known as the "Joan-Eleanor." The "Red Stocking" missions in which Edwards participated successfully gathered critical intelligence from OSS agents inside Germany that helped to hasten the war's end. After Germany's surrender, Edwards gathered intelligence on the Russians at the beginning of the Cold War.

General Donovan described OSS personnel as "glorious amateurs" who performed "some of the bravest acts of the war." I cannot think of a better description of Marvin Edwards who did much more than witness history. He made history.

Charles T. Pinck
President of the OSS Society
osssociety@aol.com

PREFACE

**RED STOCKING
(SECRET OSS MOSQUITO MISSION)**

Our de Havilland Mosquito, painted black, powered by two Rolls-Royce Merlin engines, and constructed predominantly of wood, sped through the dark sky. Due to the make of the engines, the Mosquito did not roar or vibrate as it shot silently into the night – it purred. It was April 1945 and we flew high over Germany's front-lines, the lights flickering dimly below. Equipped with a supercharger that was automatically activated at 20,000 feet, our plane was stripped of all unnecessary attachments including armament, making it possible for us to soar to 40,000 feet at a speed exceeding 400 miles per hour.

Heavy silence reigned as each of us thought of the poison pill he was to swallow should the Mosquito be shot down over Germany. We would likely be tortured to reveal what we knew if caught by the enemy, and what we knew could change the course of the war. Classified as "highly secret" and carrying the code name "Red Stocking," this perilous night flight was to be my last mission as a Mosquito navigator.

Our objective on this flight was to contact a parachuted American OSS (Office of Strategic Services) spy deep inside Germany. The 492nd Bomb Group that I was attached to was the air-arm of the OSS (predecessor of the Central Intelligence Agency). We were based at Harrington Field in the English Midlands. Known as "The Carpetbaggers" because we ventured where we weren't welcome, our unofficial nickname was "Scarlet Pimpernels of the Air."

Only a handful of German-developed jets could catch us. Germany's air minister, Herman Goering said of the Mosquito, "I turn green with envy when I see a Mosquito. The British knock together a beautiful wooden aircraft that every piano factory over there is building."

That night, flying high above the range of German anti-aircraft fire, the air in the cockpit was heated by the powerful engines. In addition to myself and the pilot, we carried an OSS operative in the modified belly of the Mosquito. His job was to converse by a sophisticated battery-operated radio system with the agent on the ground, known as "Joe," (all OSS Operatives were known as "Joe") and discover whether rumors were true of a planned continuation of the war by heavily armed fanatical SS troops making a last-ditch stand in the Bavarian Alps. Having reached the rendezvous point and established contact, we circled within a 60-mile diameter for nearly 30 minutes while the plane's agent recorded the needed information from the "Joe." That recorded OSS conversation revealed that German forces in Bavaria had no plans to continue the fight.

The end of World War II was in sight.

DEDICATION
TO THE COURAGEOUS MEN AND WOMEN OF THE OFFICE OF STRATEGIC SERVICES

SPIES LIKE US

America's History of Espionage Began with our Founding Fathers*

As a former member of the Office of Strategic Services, I was invited in 2002 to tour the spy and intelligence museum at CIA headquarters in McLean, Va. The items on display showed the ingenuity of the intelligence agencies of the United States and other nations, both friend and foe. The exhibited pieces were like props from a James Bond movie: camouflaged listening devices, concealed cameras, hidden explosive contraptions, even utensils used to carry out assassinations. Not shown for obvious reasons were current tools for spying and sabotage.

The museum makes an important case for espionage, which was of critical importance to American patriots during the Revolutionary War. On July 26, 1777, General George Washington wrote one of his top aides, "I wish you to take every possible pain in your power; by sending twenty persons to Staten Island in whom you can confide, to obtain intelligence of the enemy's situation and numbers … what kind of troops they are, and what guards they have, their strength and where posted. The necessity of procuring good intelligence is apparent."

The Second Continental Congress created an espionage agency called The Committee of Correspondence (its name was changed in November 1775 to The Committee of Secret Correspondence). Committee members included some of our best-loved patriots, including Benjamin Franklin and Benjamin Harrison, a signer of the Declaration of Independence. The committee's functions entailed utilizing secret agents abroad, carrying out covert operations, and using codes and ciphers. They also had the power to use propaganda, open private mail and have a courier system.

Franklin's heralded French travels were actually key to the nation's espionage efforts. As a CIA publication notes, "With Franklin's arrival in France in November 1776, the vital French mission became an intelligence and propaganda center for Europe, an unofficial diplomatic presentation, a coordinating facility for aid from America's secret allies and a recruiting station for such French officers as LaFayette and Kalb."

In July 1775, Franklin and Robert Morris worked out a clandestine operation to capture a major supply of British gunpowder located in Bermuda. The arsenal was raided and the barrels of gunpowder ended up with the Patriots' army. It should be noted that Morris was also a major financier of the Revolution. John Jay was the first chief of American counterintelligence. He later became the first Chief Justice of the United States. In June 1778, Washington wanted information on a major British fort at Stony Point. Capt. Allen McLane, using a disguise, successfully entered the fort. He returned, giving Washington the information he wanted.

There were numerous American spies, few of whom receive recognition in American history textbooks. The Tories believed Enoch Crosby was a British sympathizer, but he was actually a member of the Continental Army. Capt. David Gray, posing as a deserter, became an aide to a Tory intelligence officer. He reported his findings to the American command. James Armisted, a slave, acted as though he had escaped. He carried a document that gave British General Cornwallis false information about the strength of American forces. For his contribution, he was given his freedom.

Another spy and financier of the Revolution was Haym Salomon,

captured by British authorities the same day Nathan Hale was executed. He was arrested again in Aug. 1778, according to a CIA brochure, "accused this time of being an accomplice in a plot to burn the British fleet and to destroy His Majesty's warehouses." (Salomon managed to escape before his death sentence was carried out.).

Other patriot spies included Silas Deane, Robert Townsend, Maj. John Clark, Nancy Morgan Hart, Col. Benjamin Talmadge, Dr. Joseph Warren, who gave Paul Revere his assignment, Hercules Mulligan, Capt. Eli Leavenworth, Dr. James Jay, who developed a disappearing ink, Gen. Thomas Mifflin and Capt. Charles Craig.

Today, as we celebrate the 75th Anniversary of the OSS, a unified intelligence effort continues to be required to win the war against terrorists. Successful espionage is the key.

Marvin R. Edwards

*Portions of this Dedication/article appeared in FOLIO Weekly Magazine in October 2002

ACKNOWLEDGMENTS

I gratefully acknowledge and thank the following people for making this book possible:

- My wife, Helene, for her constant love and devotion

- My children, Jeffrey, Douglas and Carolyn Edwards, for their perceptive and loving critique

- Editor Karen Mathis for referring me to Biographer Susan D. Brandenburg

- CIA Museum Director Toni Hiley for her friendship and support

- My friend Bill Becker, editor of the "Carpetbagger"

- The OSS Society Staff for their support and cooperation

- The Warriors of the OSS for their heroism in war and in peace

TABLE OF CONTENTS

FOREWORD i

PREFACE iii

DEDICATION v

ACKNOWLEDGEMENTS ix

SECTION ONE – GROWING UP IN HITLER'S SHADOW 1

SECTION TWO – NEW YORK UNIVERSITY 9

SECTION THREE – U.S. AIR FORCE 35

SECTION FOUR – OSS (OFFICE OF STRATEGIC SERVICES) 53

SECTION FIVE – CARRIER COURIER 87

SECTION SIX – BACK IN THE USA 127

SECTION SEVEN – OSS REUNION – 1993 155

SECTION EIGHT – REWARDS AND RECOGNITIONS 161

SECTION NINE – REFLECTIONS 169

ADDENDUM I 185

ADDENDUM II 201

SECTION ONE
GROWING UP IN HITLER'S SHADOW

A Youth Spent in Shadows

Born in Manhattan, New York on June 29, 1921, I grew up in the aftermath of World War I and in the ever-encroaching shadow of Adolf Hitler's Germany.

My father, Albert Herman Edwards, graduated from New York's Columbia University with a degree in mechanical engineering. During World War I, he worked for the U.S. Navy, testing torpedoes. Following the war, he was warned by one of his Columbia professors that there were few opportunities for Jews in mechanical engineering, with the exception of the paper industry.

Dad became General manager of the Long Island branch of Columbia Corrugated Company, which was based in Manhattan, manufacturing cardboard boxes. Columbia Corrugated Company, with its five branches, eventually became National Container Corporation (listed on the New York Stock Exchange). When National Container Corporation realized the wood they needed for paper was growing in the southern United States, they opened paper mills in Jacksonville, Florida and Valdosta, Georgia.

Because Dad had been a successful manager on Long Island, he was transferred to Jacksonville in 1940 to take over all the negotiations with the National Paper Makers Union on behalf of National Container Corporation. Albert Edwards was known as one of the toughest, but also one of the fairest negotiators. He was also direct. As discussion got underway, he would tell the others, "I'll give you the items that are not negotiable, but everything else is negotiable."

SECTION ONE

He was a wonderful father, extremely generous to my brother Bob and me. Dad was highly principled and treated people with respect. Taking a lead from the famous IBM Slogan, "Think," Dad made it his own personal mantra for the National Container Corporation, handing out a large card with the following slogan written on it: "THINK THRU then FOLLOW THRU."

Albert and Blanche Edwards with their sons, Robert and Marvin - 1927

My mother, Blanche Gans Edwards, was a perfect housekeeper who loved to cook delicious meals for her family, especially roast beef, perhaps because her father had been a butcher in Germany. Mother was involved with the Red Cross during World War II.

There were negative influences around me as I grew to be a teenager; such as the corrupt politicians at Tammany Hall and the unsettled society in the aftermath of the first World War. Fortunately, I had the balance of parents who loved and respected one another, and also an extended affectionate family with many relatives on both sides. My older brother Bob and I attended public schools. My brother was studious, but I preferred extracurricular activities like visiting the Museum of Natural History a couple of blocks away, reading about space and astronomy, and listening to classical music.

Summers were spent with my cousin, Mauri Edwards, and my friend, Gerald Moch, at Camp Kiowa in Honesdale, Pennsylvania. There I tried to be a baseball star, but didn't make it because I had a problem with depth perception and couldn't seem to hit the ball.

Marvin, Irving & Gerald Moch, and Cousin Mauri
Camp Kiowa

SECTION ONE

Having listened with great enjoyment to classical music, I eagerly joined the camp chorus, only to be told by the chorus director that I should go through the motions but keep my mouth shut! It was a boys' camp, but there was a girls' camp, Crystal Lake, nearby. A couple of times during the summers, the camps would get together for dances. I didn't dance well, but it was just refreshing to see girls for a change.

Current events fascinated me, especially politics and global issues. I could discuss them with my father, but Mother didn't want to hear about anything unpleasant.

DeWitt Clinton High School

At DeWitt Clinton High School, I became a political activist, using words as my weapons in the battle for truth, justice and world peace. By the time I was 16, I was researching recent history and writing articles for the school newspaper that outlined my predictions for the future.

Essay dated November 12, 1937, written when I was 16 years old:

LOOKING TOWARDS THE FUTURE
By Marvin R. Edwards

It has been readily admitted time and time again by leading historians that the outlook of the world today is a very discouraging one. What are the underlying causes of the new threats against world peace? There has been such a wide range of opinion as to the cause of war that Mr. and Mrs. Average Citizen have come to the conclusion that the fundamental reasons are: Nationalism, Imperialism, Militarism and Dictatorships, with stress being put on the

latter one. All of these can be boiled down to two things: Selfishness and greed.

Looking in a standard dictionary the word selfishness is defined: "Regarding one's own comfort in disregard for others." In Spain the revolt certainly would have been put down almost as soon as it started had it not been for the help given General Franco and his rebels by Germany and Italy for purely selfish reasons. Both Hitler and Mussolini are looking forward to a Fascist Europe and if General Franco wins it should be a great blow to all of the governments of Europe, democratic or otherwise. Germany and Italy have always had their eye on the weaker countries in Europe to build up a Fascist Empire. Already parts of Spain are being occupied by the two countries. In the case of Germany, one must study more than its government to find the cause of its aggressiveness.

Before the World War, Germany had been the second greatest industrial country in Europe. She was England's only real competitor in obtaining a world market. She had money, much land in Europe, and many colonies throughout the world in which she obtained minerals and raw materials. At the end of the World War it had been expected that Germany was to be compelled to have a democratic form of government, some of her colonies taken away, some land taken and she would have to pay a reasonably large indemnity to the Allied Powers. Instead of this, by the Treaty of Versailles, Germany was forced to pay an indemnity that was so large that she almost went bankrupt. The Central Powers were forced to disarm while the Allies were not. Germany lost all her colonies and thus lost all her natural resources. About one sixth of her land in Europe was taken

SECTION ONE

away. The Weimer Republic was formed right after the war but because of the restrictions imposed by the Treaty of Versailles it failed. When Hitler came into power he scrapped all of the Treaties made since the World War.

Japan is a small country with a large population. On the Japanese Islands there are very few resources and she, therefore, had no alternative but to get the land from some other country. Of course this is no excuse for her to mercilessly attack China but this is just another example of selfishness in which Japan thinks only of herself and she shows no consideration of China's territorial rights.

English Imperialism is an excellent example of selfishness at its height. Until 1839, opium, a habit-forming drug, was being sold to the Chinese by the British East India Company who cultivated the plant in India. This plant injured the health of thousands of Chinese so the Chinese Government in 1839 forbade the importation of the white poppy. Because British merchants had been making huge profits by selling this drug, Great Britain intervened and China being a weak nation, was defeated. By the Treaty of Nanking (1842), she was forced to allow the importation of opium to her people. If the English had only been a little considerate to the Chinese Government, she would have realized that there were other products that the Chinese would have bought without any injuries to their health, and there should have been no war in the Far East.

From the beginning of civilization to today, numerous strifes have been caused by the selfishness of a powerful country over a weaker one, but the main and most important reason for any war is greed. Greed has been defined as the eager desire for wealth to hoard it and many times it is obtained at the expense of others.

The Great French Revolution at the end of the Eighteenth Century could have easily been avoided. If the nobles and the clergy had been a little more lenient with the peasants and the common people, there never would have been a revolution which took away everything the nobles had.

Napoleon's lust for power was the cause of his downfall. In simple words he bit off more than he could chew. If Napoleon had not been so ambitious, he certainly would have lasted longer as Emperor of France.

The aggressiveness of Germany, Austria-Hungary, and Turkey was one of the chief reasons for the World War. Their main objective was to control Europe. Bulgaria had different reasons for joining the Central powers. In the second Balkan War, Bulgaria was torn apart by the other Balkan countries who wanted to enlarge their boundaries and by joining the aggressive countries, she hoped to gain back her lost land.

<u>A new world war is almost unavoidable with Hitler in power. One never knows what he will do next in an attempt to get back some of the land Germany lost at the end of the World War. He cannot be put out of power without a war so the world will just have to keep its fingers crossed and hope for the best.</u>

8

SECTION TWO

NEW YORK UNIVERSITY

I was 20 years old, staying with my mother's uncle, Simon Weinstock, and his family while attending New York University in March of 1941, when I wrote the following essay:

WAKE UP AMERICA
(Take Care Today, for Tomorrow May Be Too Late!)
By Marvin R. Edwards

Germany has conquered the British Isles. The Nazis now are the overlords of Europe, Great Britain and Ireland. Adolf Hitler has achieved the first step of his mad dream to become master of all the world. Italy has become a mere pawn in the hands of the Third Reich, while Russia has been forced to cede the Ukraine to Germany.

What has happened to the people of a Europe once made up of free and independent nations? The Nazi doctrines have declared that all non-German people are inferior to the Nordic race, and they therefore must work for their Aryan masters. A slavery exists that is more beastly than anything concocted during the Dark Ages. The conquered people must be led by the government, and they are, therefore, put to work at tasks until they are completely exhausted. This is done so that none of the energy gained by eating is wasted on Non-Germanic enterprises. It is the job of the police to dispose of all those who cannot, or who won't work, in the least expensive way. The men are not shot, for the Nazis believe bullets are too expensive to waste on inferior beings.

SECTION TWO

The Non-Aryan women are given some freedom if they are willing to pay the price. They are required to bear children with Aryan blood in them. The children must not know their fathers. They are to become wards of the Government, because the Aryan father will have enough to do when he raises his own pure family.

There is only one religion. It is made up of three words, "Deutschland uber alle." Germany over all. All Catholics, Protestants and Jews must repeat these words when asked their religion.

The concentration camps do a thriving business. Death is a blessing to anyone sentenced to a camp. If a person dares to think aloud or to disobey any law he is purified by Storm Troopers using the cruelest torture devised by man. The Nazis are insane in their desire to use their power to the limit. Nothing is too cowardly or dastardly in the eyes of Himmler and his Gestapo.

At this very moment the German Government is planning for their invasion of the Western Hemisphere. With England down, we must fight alone. There is nothing between Hitler and the New World. The ocean means nothing to his long range bombers...

Now you may wonder why I have painted such a gruesome picture of a German victory, even though the English aren't licked. No, I don't think the Nazis will win, if we recognize our duty. So sit back again as you were, and breathe easy. I've mentioned what might happen to all the people on the continent of Europe, to bring home the point that there is only one barrier preventing this barbarianism from reaching

our shores. That formidable fortification is Great Britain and her Empire.

I have entitled this article "Wake Up America," because too many Americans have acted like the famous "three monkeys." They refuse to hear, see or speak of evil, even though the inner forces of hate, prejudice and brutality are drawing their tentacles closer to our shores.

There are three main modes of thought on the question. The first is that of the isolationist. His belief, in simple language, is to build a high wall around our country with no windows, so that we can maintain strict neutrality. He believes that we should let the Nazis and Japanese do as they please, unless they start knocking down the high walls we so carefully built.

The second group believes in limited aid to Britain. The people falling in this group disagree on just what the limited aid is to amount to. In reality, it amounts to giving the British enough materials not to seriously hurt our defense, or to help theirs.

The third group believes in "all out aid" to the British. They believe that Britain is fighting our battles. If Germany were to win, the belief is that we would find ourselves next on the Nazi blacklist. It is my opinion that the people in this group have done the most thinking. If England were to go down, I believe that most of the things I mentioned in the beginning of this article will come true, if not all. Since it is my belief that the only solution possible to save our democracy is "all out aid" to England, I should like to give my reasons.

SECTION TWO

Today, America is not prepared to fight Germany alone. If Great Britain were to lose tomorrow, the Nazis would have a fairly free hand in South America and Canada. We have not reached the point that we can have a two ocean navy. A well-timed attack by the Germans from across the Atlantic, and the Japanese from the Pacific, would spell disaster for America. It is the British Empire in both the west and the east that prevents any such move.

Our capacity to produce arms is progressing by leaps and bounds. Once the planes, tanks, and guns are put on a mass production basis, we need not fear any nation, or combination of countries. What we need, though, is time. Time to get our factories organized to yield war materials in an endless stream. We can gain this time by giving England the supplies she needs to keep up the heroic fight against the Nazi hordes. The English have done much to get our production going, by creating the demand that has caused many of our factories to expand. The plan to give Britain "all out aid" would be made simpler by passage of the Lend Lease Bill.

The English and American people have much in common. We speak the same language and believe in the same principles of democracy. It is no more than right that we should help a sister democracy in its fight for life, especially if it is the last outpost of freedom in Europe.

Let us suppose once again that Hitler has defeated England. For the sake of agreement with the isolationist, let us suppose that the Nazis have not made any attempt at a military invasion of the Western Hemisphere. What would be the effect of a German victory over all Europe on our

economic institutions?

We could not make any trade agreements with the Germans that would be in our favor. The Nazis do not sign pacts, unless they are the only beneficiaries. The German government will break the trade treaty when it deems it no longer vital to the security of the Third Reich. The present German government has never respected a treaty with any country. If a gangster commits one crime, he may be reformed. But if he has spent his life plundering and murdering without a second thought, that man has become a hardened criminal. Therefore, any attempt to make an economic agreement with the Nazis would be suicide. We would only be following in the steps of the long list of nations that have succumbed to the treacherous wolf in sheep's clothing. Therefore, we cannot trade with a Nazified Europe.

That would not be the only effect of a German conquest of England. If it is impossible to do business with the enslaved Continent, then we must look to Latin America. These countries are still young, and they offer an excellent market for our goods. Their imports would not be limited to products "made in the United States," for Germany has already appreciated the fact that the Latin Republics offer an outlet for German goods.

Can the United States and the Third Reich do business in Latin America on an equal footing? The answer is "No." A country with well-paid labor cannot do business on the same footing as a country having slave labor. Germany would be able to produce the same goods we can, only at half the price. To ruin our export trade, the Nazis would "dump" their goods in Latin America.

SECTION TWO

The purpose of this "economic invasion" would be to undermine our economic institutions. This bloodless war, combined with sabotage and an infiltration of fifth-columnists, would be an attempt to weaken our democratic government. The chances of the attack being successful are great. Once it started there would be little we could do to prevent it from engulfing the nation in a tidal wave of disaster. A military invasion would probably follow. Hitler and the Germans have boasted of their plans to rule the whole world. There is a saying that applies today, more than at any other time in our history. "Know the truth and you shall be free." It is always better to face the hard truth than to suffer the consequences of ignorance.

There is only one sure way of seeing that this catastrophe never occurs. We must see to it that Great Britain and her Empire stay up. Many people say that this is just another imperial war, but such a statement is completely false. England had nothing to gain by fighting, but she had her liberty and freedom to lose by not resisting the advance of the barbaric Huns.

We will be no nearer war by helping Britain than by remaining neutral. When Germany decides it is time to fight us, she will think up some excuse. It shouldn't be necessary to go down the list of all the "neutral" countries devoured by the Nazis. Had all of these nations stood together, instead of letting the German war machine march over them, one by one, Nazism would never have extended from the Black Sea to the Atlantic Ocean. If we let England down now, we shall soon meet their fate. "United we stand, divided we fall."

<u>If the only way to remove the curse of Hitler from this earth</u>

<u>is war, then we must fight. We shall beat him at his own game. We do not remove danger by running away from it. The only solution is to eliminate the source.</u>

Britain needs planes, ships and tanks. It is our job to see that our Government passes laws to answer these needs. Take advantage of your rights as citizens living in America. Your congressmen and senators must be informed that a great majority of Americans favor "all out" aid to Britain as the only means of preserving our free way of life.

The free press in America plays an important part in your lives. Let your newspapers know how you stand, for the power of the pen is mighty; its influence is far reaching. When people say we shouldn't help Britain because they are already beaten, show them that we can only save ourselves by helping them. Explain to them that they are fighting our battles and the least we can do is to help them win them.

While it is the duty of our government to see that the British people get the supplies they need to carry on the war, it is our duty to see that they get the war relief so badly needed. It is not enough to say that we want Germany defeated. It is not enough to say we understand the hardships the brave people of England have undergone. Sympathy will not buy clothes or food. The most important charity work we can do now is to give to the British War Relief. There are those people who say, "Charity begins at home," and if we let England down now, we shall eventually have no homes here to give charity to. Many of us claim we haven't the money to give. This seems so selfish when the British people are giving their only lives.

SECTION TWO

> Wake up America! If you value your freedom, you must defend it. You must be willing to make sacrifices to keep the lights of liberty burning. Rise America. It shall be your duty to lay the foundation for the world of tomorrow. Twenty-three years ago you had the same opportunity, but you rejected it. John Bull [England] is giving you a chance to prepare for your mission of the future. England and the world are counting on you, Uncle Sam. Don't let them down. Wake up America! The fate of the world is in your hands.

Sadly, my predictions about a well-planned attack by the Japanese in the Pacific, were fully realized on December 7, 1941. I was living with the Weinstock family at that time. The family was out and I was at home writing a report on office management work flow and listening to the New York Philharmonic on the radio when the program was interrupted to announce that the Japanese had bombed Pearl Harbor. When the Weinstocks got home, I asked, "Did you hear the news?" They hadn't heard anything yet and when I told them the Japanese had attacked, they couldn't believe it. I was not at all surprised. I had been predicting that they would do something like that for quite some time.

In the book, <u>Pearl Harbor, Fact and Reference Book, Everything to Know about December 7, 1941</u>, by Terence McComas, published in 1991 by Mutual Publishing in Hawaii, there are some incredibly telling Q & A listings of various descriptions and predictions regarding Japan's aggressive nature. Several of those quotes from the book follow:

Q: What launched Japan into a major power?
A: A series of military victories including the Sino-Japanese War, the annexation of Korea in 1910 and the annexation

of German territories in the Pacific, and China during World War I. Japan's victory over Russia made Japan a rival with the United States and Britain for control in the Pacific.

Q: When did the United States begin to consider Japan a potential threat?
A: After Japan's gains in the Russo-Japanese War in 1905.

Q: Who said, "One day, Japan would go to war with the United States for supremacy in the Pacific?"
A: In October 1924, General Billy Mitchell made this prediction in a report to the United States War Department. He believed it would be a surprise attack by carrier-based airplanes against Pearl Harbor and Schofield Barracks. Mitchell's report was filed away and ignored.

Q: Who wrote, "It seems to me increasingly clear that we are bound to have a showdown someday, and the principle question at issue is whether it is to our advantage to have that showdown sooner or later?"
A: America's Ambassador to Japan, Joseph Grew, wrote this to President Roosevelt on December 14, 1940, because of his concern about Japan's expansionist policy.

Q: "Whether rightly or wrongly, the people of the United States seem to believe all the so-called experts' claims that Japan has only two bathtubs in the Navy, no money, no oil, and all Japanese fliers are so cross-eyed they couldn't hit Lake Michigan with a bomb." Where did this appear?
A: It was published in the Chicago Daily News. The writer

SECTION TWO

was upset about the false ideas most Americans had about Japan.

Q: Who said, "It appears that the most likely and dangerous form of attack on Oahu would be an air attack ... most likely be launched from one or more carriers, probably approach inside of 300 miles ... in a dawn attack there is a high probability that it could be delivered as a complete surprise"?

A: In March 1941, Major General Frederick Martin, commander of the Hawaii Army Air Corps, and Rear Admiral Patrick L. N. Bellinger, Commander of the Hawaii Naval Air Patrol, filed this joint report.

Q: When and how did the United States government first warn Hawaii about a possible attack?

A: Secretary Knox signed a letter on January 24, 1941, warning, "Japan might initiate a surprise attack upon the fleet at Pearl harbor. Military commanders in Hawaii are to take every step, as quickly as possible, to protect against the attack."

Q: "Here in Hawaii we all live in a citadel or gigantically fortified island." Who said this?

A: Lieutenant General Walter Short, Commanding General, Hawaiian Department, in a speech on April 7, 1941.

Q: Who made the following statement: "Pearl Harbor is the strongest Fortress in the world ... a major attack is impractical"?

A: In May 1941, Army Chief of Staff, General George C. Marshall, gave this description to President Roosevelt.

Q: Who said, "We can't go to war because we aren't ready to go to war?"
A: A statement made by General George C. Marshall shortly before the attack on Pearl Harbor.

Q: Who said, "Japanese sanity cannot be measured by our standards of logic."?
A: Ambassador Grew's message on 3 November to the United States State Department as he tried to explain Japan's "Do or Die" attitude, rather than give in to foreign pressure.

Q: Who said, "The United States Navy can defeat the Japanese Navy at any place, at any time"?
A: A statement made by Senator Owen Brewster of Maine while he was at the Naval Air Station in San Juan, Puerto Rico on December 4, 1941.

Q: Who said, "The American people may feel fully confident in their Navy ... on any comparable basis the United States Navy is second to none"?
A: Secretary of the Navy Frank Knox's report on the United States Navy, given on December 6, 1941.

Q: Who sent the following message: "Japanese are presenting on one p.m. eastern standard time today what amounts to an ultimatum. Also they are under orders to destroy their code machines immediately. Just what significance the hour set may have we do not know but be on the alert accordingly. Inform naval authorities of this communication"?
A: A warning message sent by General Marshall, at 11:58 Eastern Standard Time on December 7, 1941, to Lieutenant General Short.

SECTION TWO

FACT: By 1940, Admiral Yamamoto began to think of offensive strategies. He was influenced by Hector C. Bywater and Homer Lea. Hector Bywater published a book called <u>The Great Pacific War</u>. In it, Bywater discussed war strategies in the Pacific, and predicted Japan would make a surprise attack on Pearl Harbor, as well as Guam and the Philippines. Yamamoto studied the book and used many of Bywater's strategies. If Yamamoto had not been influenced by Bywater, he may have decided on an initial attack on the Dutch East Indies instead of Pearl Harbor. Had that happened, the United States' interest and participation in the conflict would have been very different. Homer Lea published a fictional history in 1909 describing Japanese plans to conquer the United States. The book, <u>The Valor of Ignorance</u>, predicted that the Japanese could easily take the Philippines, Hawaii and Alaska and gain control of the northern Pacific. The Japanese also published Lea's book, calling it <u>The War Between Japan and America</u>. It caught the interest of military on both sides.

As a student of history and one who has made several predictions of events that actually occurred, I am sometimes surprised by the realization that there are many historical students and military experts who have made similar prognostications, all to no avail. I was writing articles and focusing on current events and thinking about the future, all the time knowing that I would eventually enter the fray. In the meantime, I did what I could do for the war effort while trying to complete my goals for higher education.

The Weinstocks' home was right across the street from where Poet Edgar Allen Poe had once lived. It was also located in a strategic position facing the Grand Concourse, where there were controls

for the street lights in the neighborhood. Because I lived in an attic room, I became a volunteer Air Raid Warden and served in that capacity during 1941 and 1942 until after I enlisted in the Air Force. Assigned to facing the Grand Concourse, I learned certain signals during practices that turned the lights on or off in case of attack. It was key to control the street lights so that enemy bombers would not be able to find their targets. Although we never suffered an attack, we were deadly serious about our drills and blackouts because the fear of another Pearl Harbor style raid was always on our minds.

PRODUCTION – The Magazine of Facts at NYU

I became editor of PRODUCTION Magazine, published by the Management Club at New York University. I asked my friend, Ellis Somech, to be co-editor with me. As an Iranian Jew, he was virtually ignored by many at the University because of his ethnicity and thick accent.

At PRODUCTION Magazine, we attempted to include business and industrial analyses by some of America's most prominent businessmen and reached out for articles and commentary by our nation's leaders. We learned that most of the leaders were accessible, so I was never intimidated by celebrities and political figures after that experience.

For instance, we requested an article from Senator Harry S. Truman, Chair of the U.S. Senate Committee on Interstate Commerce. Senator Truman responded with the following letter:

SECTION TWO

> **United States Senate**
> COMMITTEE ON INTERSTATE COMMERCE
>
> Washington, D. C.
> March 5, 1942
>
> Mr. Marvin Edwards
> Management Club, New York University
> Washington Square
> New York City
>
> Dear Mr. Edwards:
>
> I appreciate very much your invitation to write an article for the forthcoming issue of your official magazine PRODUCTION.
>
> It is not possible for me to write such an article for your magazine at the present time. I am enclosing you a copy of my Committee's report to the Senate, and if there is any part which you would like to publish in your magazine you are perfectly welcome to do it.
>
> It expresses my views on the present conditions, and the past, as we found them.
>
> Sincerely yours,
>
> Harry S. Truman, U. S. S.
>
> HST:MLD
> encl.

Among some of the articles that ran in our May 7, 1942 edition were "Radio in Wartime," by David Sarnoff, president of the Radio Corporation of America; H. V. Kaltenborn's dissension about the challenging aspects of Defense; and a message to businessmen by General Lewis B. Hershey, director of Selective Service. The May 7th issue was dedicated to a former NYU student who had joined the Air Force, Lt. Frank G. J. Micieli, "recently killed in an airplane crash."

PRODUCTION Magazine Editor Marvin Edwards & Staff (1942)

On Monday, October 19, 1942, we announced in the New York University Commerce Bulletin that PRODUCTION Magazine, in a revised form, would make its appearance on December 1, attempting to show how one year of war had affected the civilian population, especially college students, and the kind of world we could expect when the war was over. In conjunction with that attempt, we requested articles from Henry J. Kaiser, the miracle ship-builder, Major Alexander P. Seversky, author of "Victory Through Air Power," Pearl Buck, well-known author and lecturer on the Far East; Paul V. McNutt, chairman of the Manpower Commission; Milo Perkins, director of the Board of Economic Warfare; and William Ziff, author of "The Coming Battle for Germany."

I received letters of response from nearly all of the people I contacted, most of the people expressing their regrets that they were unable to accommodate me with an article at this time due to

SECTION TWO

time constraints. It was, after all, war-time. However, there were several well-known people who did give me permission to publish previously written articles in our paper. Hanson W. Baldwin, one of the New York Times' top writers, sent me the following letter:

> The New York Times
> Times Square
>
> March 4, 1942
>
> Mr. Marvin Edwards
> Management Club - New York University
> School of Commerce, Accounts and Finance
> Washington Square
> New York, N.Y.
>
> Dear Mr. Edwards:
>
> Much as I should like to contribute to the forthcoming issue of PRODUCTION, I am afraid that it is out of the question for me to undertake anything more at the present time. The month of March is going to be a very heavy one for me and I see no possibility of enough free moments to do the article you would like though I particularly would like to contribute to the Navy Relief Drive. If it should come within the scope of your editorial policy you might, however, be able to find something of particular pertinence in my Times articles or in articles in other publications I have written in the past. If so, you are at liberty to reprint from them so long as proper credit is given to the publication.
>
> Sincerely yours,
>
> Hanson W. Baldwin
> Military and Naval Correspondent

Baldwin's letter was more heartfelt, but somewhat typical of the letters I received in response to my requests. As I said, I attempted to get feedback from as many leaders as I could, including President Franklin D. Roosevelt:

> THE WHITE HOUSE
> WASHINGTON
>
> March 3, 1942
>
> Dear Mr. Edwards:
>
> This acknowledges your letter of February twenty-sixth, requesting an article by the President for inclusion in the forthcoming issue of PRODUCTION. I regret to advise you that it will not be possible for the President to comply with your request. May I explain that ever since he has been in his present position the President has followed a course of not expressing his views exclusively in any publication. As he has not deviated from this course, I am sure you will appreciate the difficulty of making an exception in this instance and will excuse him.
>
> Very sincerely yours,
>
> *Stephen Early*
> STEPHEN EARLY
> Secretary to the President
>
> Mr. Marvin Edwards,
> Co-Editor, PRODUCTION,
> Management Club,
> New York University,
> Washington Square,
> New York, N. Y.

On November 9, 1942, the Commerce Bulletin ran an article about me with the headline "Dictator Tide Prophesied by Management Student." The article was actually an editorial about me written by me (being the editor allowed me to do that). The editorial read as follows:

> Unusual pastimes have been cropping up all over Commerce lately, but this is the first time we've come across one that is really worth the time it demands.

SECTION TWO

For the past six years, Marvin Edwards, a management major, has been industriously collecting articles and reading books on the rise of Nazism and the Japanese war lords. When he started with his hobby, he had ambitions of being a writer of foreign affairs someday.

As far back as 1936, he wrote that unless the democracies would band together, they would find themselves snowed under by the rising tide of dictatorships. He further stated that the Japanese were planning a conquest of all Asia.

"The Japanese desire to conquer is not new," Edwards declared. "It began about 2000 years ago, when the first groups to settle in Japan fought amongst themselves. Since that time, Japan has been constantly fighting Asiatic mainland – in most cases the aggressors.

"Japan declared war on Germany in 1914, knowing that she would not have much to do with the actual fighting end. She wanted the spoils of war – all German islands in the Pacific. And at the end of the last war, the Japanese were given a mandate over all German islands north of the equator, since they had seized them anyway. The Japanese were already thinking about December 7, 1941."

Edwards has expressed surprise that most of the students at New York U. know practically nothing about the countries we are fighting, especially Japan, and the kind of philosophy the people in these countries have. He has also found that too many of the students are rather ill-informed about the strategic importance of many key points and their location in this war of world-wide geographic proportions.

On Monday, November 23, 1942, my article, "This is Japan's Asia", appeared in the Commerce Bulletin:

> Japanese troops were at the gates of Nanking, December 13, 1937. The civilians and soldiers within the city braced themselves for the coming attack. The enemy decided not to storm the city. Instead, Japanese planes flew over and dropped leaflets on the city telling the Chinese to lay down their arms and surrender. The pamphlets further stated that no harm would come to anyone if they offered no resistance. Believing the Japanese, the people opened up the gates at Nanking.
>
> The events that followed during the next two weeks will long live in infamy. First, the Japanese seized all the arms and rounded up the Chinese soldiers. Next, the invaders looted every wine cellar and drank the contents of every bottle they could find. Satisfied that they had their fill, the Chinese soldiers were brutally murdered. They were tied to poles and the Japanese practiced bayonetting.
>
> After this taste of blood, the Japanese soldiers went through every house, raped the women, killed the old men and children and then set the homes on fire. The drunken invaders were still not satisfied.
>
> They remembered that they had forgotten the students at the University of Nanking. The Japanese believed these educated boys constituted a menace to their homeland. Hundreds of the students were seized and tied together in groups of fifty. Gasoline was poured over each group, and the Japanese threw lighted matches on them. Hundreds of college students were burned alive.

SECTION TWO

The action of the Japanese at Nanking has been repeated to a lesser degree in all the territory under Japan's domination. English and American civilians were mistreated by the Japanese for many years before their attack on Pearl Harbor. The Westerners were beaten for no reason at all. American and English men and women were compelled to undress in public under the pretext of receiving orders to be searched. The Japanese never stated just what they were looking for.

In order to keep the conquered people in complete submission, the Japanese government has devised a fiendish plan. It is compulsory for the subjugated people to use narcotics. By this method the Japanese hope to weaken the minds and spirit of their victims, and force them to turn to Japan for a continued supply of drugs. This is how our Nipponese enemy is laying plans for his "Asia for the Asiatics."

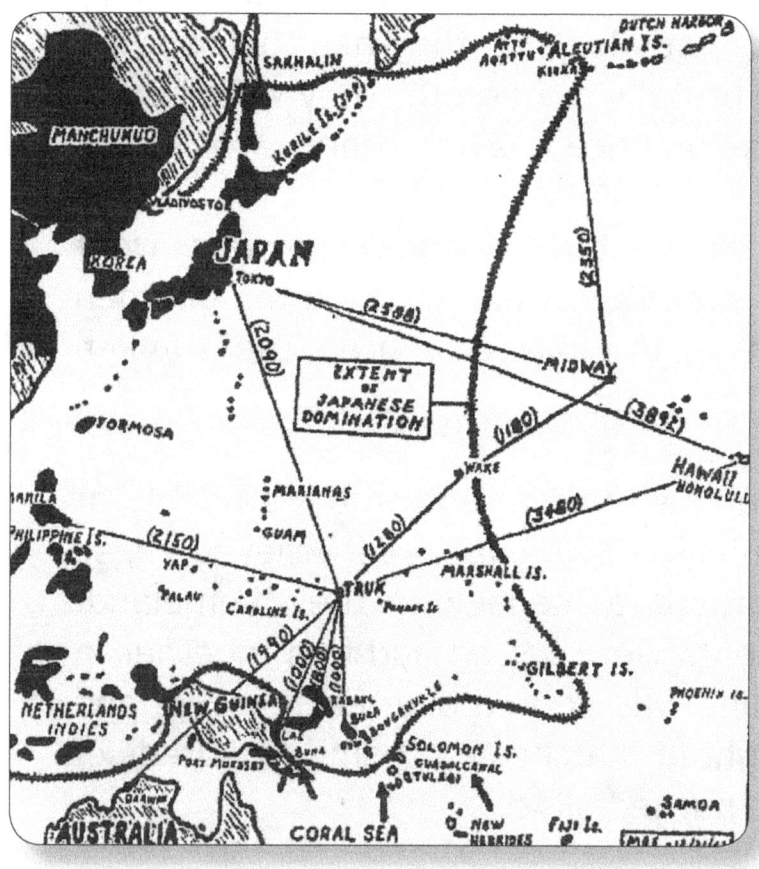

In December of 1942, after a great deal of research, I wrote an article about Truk for PRODUCTION Magazine, published by the Management Club of New York University. To further illustrate my research and prediction regarding Truk, I drew a map depicting the Truk Islands.

Truk – Japan's Pearl Harbor
By Marvin R. Edwards

Truk is the key bastion for all Japanese offensive and defensive operations in the South Pacific. This island group has often been referred to as the Japanese Hawaiian Islands. The importance of Truk and its adjacent islands was recognized by Japanese militarists more than a quarter of a century ago.

In August 1914, the Japanese declared war against Germany with the express purpose of seizing the then weakly fortified German territory in the Far East. Within a few weeks, Nipponese forces were in control of the German Marianas, Marshall, and Caroline Islands. Truk is part of the Carolines.

By clever political maneuvering, the Japanese were awarded a Class C mandate over these and other German Islands north of the equator. The Class C mandate was virtually outright annexation. The only restriction was that these islands were not to be fortified. The Japanese agreed to this ruling. Then they started to fortify the newly acquired mandates.

Most maps represent Truk as a single dot in the Pacific. Actually, an enlargement shows it to be about 20 volcanic isles surrounded by a coral reef. The area enclosed by the reef is more than 400 square miles, of which, the most important islands are Dublon and Eten.

Dublon has one of the best natural harbors in the Pacific. It has facilities to dock, repair, and service vessels as large as battleships. It is the most important Japanese naval base

SECTION TWO

south of Tokyo.

Eten is a smaller island just south of Dublon. It is used as an air base for Japanese bombers and fighter planes patrolling the area.

When we read of Japanese fleet movements near the Solomons, New Guinea, or Midway, the chances are that the vessels were based at Truk. The fleet we routed in recent engagements in the Solomon area originated at Truk. It was observed fleeing back toward that base.

The Truk group is strategically located. It is protected from surprise attack by hundreds of Japanese controlled islands extending for a thousand miles in all directions. No American task force could slip through without being spotted long before it reached its objective. Even those islands that are too small to serve as military bases are used as observation posts to warn of any approaching attack. If we were able to fight our way through the protecting coral reef that extends around this island group, there are only four passes through the reef. Each is well guarded. <u>There is only one way of bypassing the reef; that is by destroying the usefulness of Truk by bombing.</u>

Truk is closer to the south Pacific battle fronts than our naval and air bases at Hawaii. It is only 1,500 miles to the northwest of Guadalcanal in the Solomons, while Pearl Harbor is about 3,500 miles northeast of the Solomons. Truk is 1,000 miles north of Lae in New Guinea.

As the battle for the south Pacific grows more intense, Truk will appear more and more in the headlines.

The Undersea World of Jacques Cousteau, airing in 1971 (some 27 years later), dramatically proved that my dire prediction was realized by 1944.

On October 20, 1942, shortly before I enlisted in the Army Air Force, I wrote the following article for PRODUCTION Magazine, titled "The Battleship is Obsolete":

> The superiority of the plane over the battleship is recognized today. It might have been twenty-two years ago, that is, if tradition hadn't triumphed over common sense. In a speech before a Senate Committee in 1920, General Billy Mitchell said, "Battleships opposed by aircraft will become as obsolete as plumed knights after the invention of gunpowder."
>
> The present World War is more than three years old. During that time, battleships have made the front page only under two circumstances: when they are launched and when they are sunk.

SECTION TWO

The time it takes to build a modern battleship is three or four years. The cost is well over one-hundred million dollars. Aside from the cost and the time, many vital materials and manpower, that might be used for some immediate projects, are used up.

The believers in the "old tub" have been defending it with a theory that is as obsolete as the battleship. They claim that there is no other weapon that has as much of a concentrated fire as the battlewagon. No one will deny this statement. The answer is, that in this war, the battleship does not get a chance to use its full power. There have only been two instances in which a battleship is known to have engaged other warships. The first was in a running battle off South America in which the Graf Spee was made so ineffective that it was scuttled by its crew. Air power played no part in this battle. The other contest between warships was off the French Coast. In this fight, the Bismarck landed one of its first shots into the magazine of the Hood. (The British called it a lucky hit). The Hood was blown up, but the pride of the German Navy didn't escape. It was spotted by a patrol plane, and then it was crippled by British torpedo planes. In order to save face, for the whole British Navy was looking for the warship to avenge the Hood, a few warships were given the privilege of sending the Bismarck to the bottom.

The score thus far is, three battleships mentioned, and three battleships sunk. Let's look at some of the other battlewagons that have received mention in the press.

There was the 35,000-ton battleship Prince of Wales, and the 32,000-ton battle cruiser Repulse. They both were new ships, that is, until Japanese torpedo planes sent them to a

watery grave. They never had a chance to fire their 16 inch guns, only anti-aircraft guns.

Other battleships have received mention in the paper. There was the Japanese warship sent to the bottom by a flying fortress piloted by Collin Kelly. At Pearl Harbor we lost the old battlewagons, Arizona and Oklahoma to Japanese dive bombers and torpedo planes. In the battle of Midway, three Japanese aircraft carriers were lost, two were damaged, and three heavy cruisers were also hit. All by air-power. In the Coral Sea engagement and battle of Midway, the surface ships never got within range of each other. In fact, there had been no naval engagement with the Japanese, except where land based planes and carrier planes did all of the fighting. The ships did nothing except to stand, or float in the water, and to take punishment.

Battleships have done nothing in this war to warrant the time, money, effort, and materials that are put into them. As the range and power of the sky destroyers increases, the chances of the battleship to be a deciding factor in this war will decrease.

If a battleship has a blanket of planes over head, then it may be able to float, and to fight. But the question then arises, that the aircraft overhead might do better if it were not tied down to defensive purposes. The blanket of planes over the ship could probably accomplish everything the battleship set out to do.

The battleship is a weapon of the last war. The plane and the submarine have made it an easy target. Its existence is due to the sentiment of old time Navy men, in this country

SECTION TWO

and in the other Naval powered countries. In wartime there is no time for such sentiment.

SECTION THREE

AIR FORCE

I was a senior at New York University's School of Commerce, Accounts and Finance in late 1942 when I enlisted in the Army Air Force, planning to be trained as a pilot. There were military recruiters at the University and I volunteered for the Army Air Force rather than the Navy because I felt that being in an airplane was better than being a sitting target on a ship. As I wrote about and watched the progression of the war in both the European and Pacific Theatres, I felt I had a duty to fight for my country. Although I knew of the atrocities happening to Jews, including relatives who remained in Germany rather than fleeing, my main motivation for volunteering was my love for my country. I resolved to become the best American soldier I could be.

The University said that any seniors remaining at school until March 31, 1943 would be given their diploma and considered a graduate, but since I'd been told by the Air force that I would be called to active duty in February, I did not return to N.Y.U. after the December holiday break. As it turned out, I was not called up until April 5th. Thus, after my time in the service, I had to return to the University to get my degree, finally graduating in 1947.

That incident with scheduling, even before reporting for duty, taught me a lesson on how the military worked. I vowed that I would train and learn to the best of my ability to serve my country, however, I would also get involved in extracurricular activities wherever possible, thus exercising some control over my destiny as well as earning some special privileges.

Having enlisted in the U.S. Army Air Force just before the winter holiday break at NYU, I spent a great deal of time waiting, thinking

SECTION THREE

and researching ... and writing, writing, writing!

In January of 1943, while waiting to be called up, I wrote long essays on Japan's history, as well as some political commentaries on the global situation. In an article titled "Japan, Scourge of the Far East," I wrote about the history of Japanese-American relations, describing the general lack of knowledge about Japan by the average American and the fact that the Japanese were a warring nation, having been fighting since 660 B.C. I wrote about our discomfort with Japanese aggression and the protests that had been made repeatedly by our United States Ambassador to Japan, Joseph C. Grew, all to no avail. The following paragraphs are excerpted from that essay:

> In December 1937 the U.S.S. Panay was bombed and strafed, while in the Yangtze River, by Japanese planes even though the vessel was plainly marked with a large American flag painted on the deck. As usual there were apologies and small indemnities but similar situations continued to occur.
>
> In July 1939 our government taking long delayed action gave notice to Japan of the termination of the commercial treaty with Japan that was signed in 1911. This termination removed the legal obstacle to the embargo by the U.S. upon the shipment of materials to Japan, who was using them to build up her military might. According to the State Department's White Paper released January 1943, the U.S. Ambassador in Japan cabled to the Secretary of State on September 12, 1940 "... that whatever the intentions of the existing Japanese government there could be no doubt that the military and other elements in Japan saw in the world situation a 'golden opportunity' to carry their dreams of expansion into effect; that the German victories, like

strong wine had gone to their heads; that they had believed implicitly until recently in Great Britain's defeat; that they had argued that the war would probably be ended in a quick German victory and that Japan's position in greater East Asia should be consolidated while Germany was still agreeable and that discounted effective composition on our part."

In September 1940 following an ultimatum which threatened the use of force, Japanese troops occupied part of French Indo-China, the purpose being to gain new bases for operations against China, and to lay the foundation for any future moves in the South Pacific.

Ambassador Grew reported to the Department of State on January 27th, 1941, that one of his diplomatic colleagues had told a member of the embassy staff that there were reports from many sources, including a Japanese source, that Japanese military forces planned a surprise mass attack at Pearl Harbor in case of "trouble" with the United States.

On September 27, 1940, Germany, Italy and Japan signed a 10-year military and economic alliance, promising mutual assistance if any of them became involved in a war with any power "not yet belligerent." The pact was directed at the U.S., of course. Still trying to reach mutual understanding and achieve peace in the Far East, we welcomed the arrival in Washington of the new Japanese ambassador Admiral Nomura in March 1941, and special envoy Saburo Kurusu on November 16, 1941. Conferences with Japanese representatives were still going on when Pearl Harbor was bombed at 7:50 a.m. on December 7, 1941. Fourteen hours later, the U.S. Embassy at Tokyo received a communication from the Japanese foreign minister informing the

SECTION THREE

Ambassador that "There has arisen a state of war between your Excellency's country and Japan beginning today."

I also wrote about the popular term "Second Front," that was being bandied about by nearly every country during those turbulent war years, arguing that there was no meaning to the term because there were simultaneous "fronts" occurring throughout the world. There were at least four active fronts in Asia and the Pacific, two in Europe and two in Africa, in addition to fighting at fronts yet to be conquered, such as Yugoslavia. I noted that the term "second front" had originated in Russia, the original idea being to open another front against Germany to draw German troops from the already strained Russian front. Avidly devouring every bit of news from all the "fronts," I wrote about the African campaign, "Our military leaders knew that a new front had to be opened, but they had to wait until the right time, regardless of public opinion. An invasion of Africa before we were completely prepared would have been suicidal. As careful as we were in planning the African campaign, the Germans still were able to land a formidable force in Tunisia, and Rommel was able to retreat in fairly good order for 2,000 miles, after his original setback."

I concluded, "The term 'second front' cannot be defined. It grew out of a fear that the united nations were content to sit back and fight a defensive war. We know this is no longer true, for we have opened new fronts in the Pacific and African theatres of war. It is the Axis that is now on the defensive, and their people do not look forward to new fronts with the same feeling. We wanted them because we didn't think we were doing enough, while the Axis nations know it means the beginning of the end."

My faith in the strength and courage of my fellow countrymen and in the expected outcome of our nation in World War II was

bolstered greatly in January of 1943 by the State of the Union Address of President Franklin D. Roosevelt. I wrote an editorial about it, submitting it to the morning paper on January 8, 1943. That article follows in its entirety:

THE STATE OF THE UNION
(EDITORIAL ON PRESIDENT ROOSEVELT'S
ADDRESS TO CONGRESS JAN. 7, 1943)
Submitted to the New York Herald Tribune

President Franklin D. Roosevelt entered the halls of Congress yesterday morning amid the greatest ovation he has received since he first assumed office in 1932. The occasion was the deliverance of his message to the new Seventy-Eighth Congress. The address was a report to Congress and the American people on the "State of the Union."

The message has been hailed by our political leaders, and those of the other united nations as having a unifying influence on all of the peoples fighting the Axis. There was no one note of discord in the speech that anyone could say would create dissension among our ranks. The President praised our fighting men, as well as the unconquerable spirit of our allies, especially China, Russia and England. With only two exceptions, the speech dealt in generalities and facts already known. This was not a fault, for an enlarged discussion of our gains in production, or of our next objectives on the battlefronts would be of more use to the enemy than to us. The exceptions were in the releasing of certain broad production figures and in our aid to China.

Speaking of our 1942 production, the President said that we built 8,090,000 tons of merchant shipping. This was greater

SECTION THREE

than the goal set. "We produced 56,000 combat vehicles, such as tanks and self-propelled artillery." We produced 670,000 machine guns and 21,000 anti-tank guns, six times greater than our 1941 production. "We produced ten and a quarter billion rounds of small arms ammunition and 181 million rounds of artillery ammunition." The President said, "these facts and figures will give no aid and comfort to the enemy." He is certainly right in that statement. The enemy may well wonder how he could have ever believed that American industry couldn't be counted on to deliver the goods of destruction as well as of peace. These production figures give us good reason to be optimistic. However, we must remember that no mention was made of how much of these materials are overseas. While our ship building has exceeded our goals, the problem of shipping and the submarine menace to our supply lines, still constitute a major problem.

The other surprising statement made by the President was that, "We are flying as much Lend-lease material to China as ever transversed the Burma Road." This either means that we have never sent China much in the way of supplies, or else our air transport system is accomplishing much more than we had been led to believe. We can only hope that the second statement is true.

The last half of the Chief-Executive's message dealt with the objectives that we are striving for in the post-war world, namely the Four Freedoms. He reiterated his belief that there would only be an era of peace and good will if they were carried out. The President reassured the boys in uniform that there will be "no get-rich-quick era of bogus prosperity which will end for them in selling apples on a

street corner, as happened after the bursting of the boom in 1929." This statement of Freedom from Want certainly will help to bolster the morale of many servicemen who have been wondering what kind of country they would be coming back to.

The President warned us that "a tremendous, costly, long-enduring task in peace as well as in war is still ahead of us." "But," he continued, "as we face that continuing task, we may know that the state of this Nation is good – the heart of this Nation is sound – the spirit of this Nation is strong – the faith of this Nation is eternal." He may have added, for this is America, and we are Americans.

I finally reported for active duty in April 1943 at Moody Air Force Base in Valdosta, Georgia. After a short stay, I was sent off to Keesler Field in Biloxi, Mississippi, where I spent four weeks in basic training. Today, Biloxi is a busy gambling community, but back then Keesler Field in Biloxi was a hell hole. Everyone in our squadron developed a bad cough that hung on even after we left. The nicest comment heard there was, "Keesler was the only place one could be knee deep in mud and have sand blowing in your face."

NEW CADET 4/43

Marvin R. Edwards, son of Mr. and Mrs. Albert H. Edwards, of 1103 River Oaks road, has been ordered to active duty as an aviation cadet with the Army Air Force. His assignment will take him to Biloxi, Miss., for pre-aviation cadet training.

Edwards was a senior at the School of Commerce, Accounts, and Finance of New York university when he was first advised of his call to active duty. He has a brother, Lt. Robert D. Edwards in the Army Ordnance, who is now stationed in St. Louis, Mo.

My next assignment was at a college training detachment at Dickinson College located in

SECTION THREE

Carlisle, Pennsylvania. While there, we took refresher courses in algebra and trigonometry. We also took preliminary courses in astronomy and meteorology. Finally, we began our flying training using Piper Cub aircraft.

Mayor Alsop of Jacksonville was a friend of our family. He wrote a letter of introduction to my commanding officer at Dickinson, which must certainly have gone a long way toward my being appointed editor of the station newspaper.

I wrote a war analysis for the station newspaper at Dickinson and, before long, became editor. The major in charge was associated with the Hoover War Library at Stanford University in Palo Alto, California. He had copies of the paper sent there and was happy to have his picture taken each time dignitaries visited the detachment. We became good friends and I was granted off-base passes in appreciation (a great example of how extracurricular activities resulted in special privileges). The war analysis, titled "Trend of Our War with Japan", pointed out the two phases of the war in the Pacific, the first phase being the

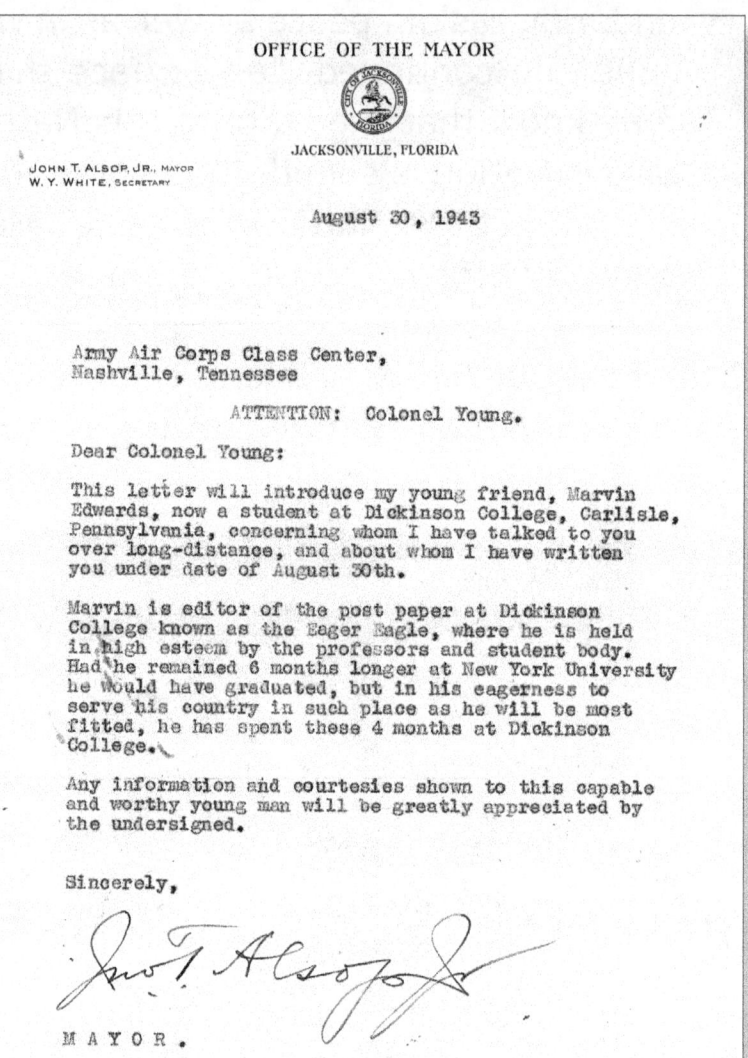

period from December 7, 1941 to June 4, 1942, when Japan met little opposition as they occupied nearly one-quarter of the globe. The second phase of our war with Japan began with the Battle of Midway. I compared Japan's defeat at Midway to the eventual results of a persistent man attempting to break up a large boulder by hitting it with a strong club. "He hits the rock many times, but only small chips seem to be breaking off. The man becomes a little discouraged, but he decides to strike the rock with one more heavy blow. He brings his club all the way over his shoulder and brings it down on the rock with everything he can put behind it. The rock is smashed into a million pieces. Each blow had helped to weaken the rock along its fault lines, though it wasn't very noticeable. The final blow proved too much for the already weakened rock, but its destruction was the result of all the blows combined. And in the same manner, our blows against the Japanese Navy and Air Force don't seem to have any noticeable effect from the outside, but the inner workings of the Japanese military probably are feeling it." They most certainly were feeling it, as it later turned out that the Battle of Midway was the downward turning point in the war for Japan.

From Carlisle, I was sent to Maxwell Field in Montgomery, Alabama. Here I received additional schooling prior to going to the Mississippi Institute of Aeronautics in Jackson, Mississippi where I had my primary flying

SECTION THREE

training. There, as often seemed to happen, I started writing a column for the station newspaper and soon became senior editor. Although my penchant for journalism continued strong, sadly, my hopes to become a pilot were dashed.

During some rolling and spin maneuvers on a practice flight, I developed vertigo and was advised I would do better as a navigator on a bomber. I was frustrated and disappointed to lose the chance to be a fighter pilot, but I knew I couldn't argue about it. In fact, my family had already expressed their doubts about my ability to pilot an airplane, kidding me because I used to get dizzy in the New York subway!

I was transferred to a reclassification center at Nashville, Tennessee, where I took a series of tests and was told I was well-qualified to be a navigator. Navigation School at Selman field in Monroe, Louisiana was my next stop.

Navigation School involved a four-month course which included flight missions to practice what we learned. We were trained in celestial navigation which we felt was not too practical for fast-flying aircraft, although it was fine for ships. There was a heavily guarded building that had radar equipment which we were told was "hush hush." Later, when I arrived at Harrington, I found out that both the Germans and the British had been using radar for navigation for some time. During my entire stay in Europe, I used celestial navigation only once, and that was when the radar installation on the B-24 failed while over Germany, and I had to get a fix on the stars to find our way back to England. I was grateful, then (and so was my crew) that I had been trained so well and scored so high on that aspect of navigational training. There was never a moment's doubt that I could navigate by the stars.

While at Selman Field, I wrote a series of articles on the history of Japan and how, step by step, they had laid the groundwork for an eventual war with America. In researching the articles, I became familiar, for the first time, with an incredibly prophetic writer and philosopher named Homer Lea.* His writings would continue to intrigue and inspire me for the rest of my life.

The following article reveals a lot about the Japanese mentality and why they approached war from such a radical perspective. The introduction, a quote from Homer Lea, was written many decades before the Japanese bombed Pearl Harbor ... amazing!

1944 Article in "True Drift"
published by the Monroe News Star -- World Publishing Corp
furnished by Selman Field Public Relations Office
for general release
By Marvin R. Edwards

Now that the military campaign in Europe has reached its decisive stage, our eyes turn to the west, and more directly to the Island Empire of Japan, with its tentacles embracing almost half a billion people.

Until war came, few of us had any interest, and cared less about the beliefs that motivate the Japanese in their thoughts and actions. A study of the inherent characteristics of the Japanese people, their emperor, and the mythical origin about which their lives revolve, can provide the key to the seemingly incomprehensible Japanese mind.

Emperor Hirohito is not looked upon as an ordinary earthly being. He is the 128th direct descendant of Amaterasu, the Sun Goddess. A fairy tale to us, but the motivating spirit of

*ADDENDUM I – Homer Lea – Biography and Quotes

SECTION THREE

80,000,000 Japanese. The state religion of Shintoism; the sun symbol on their flag; the many rituals that are blended into their daily lives, have maintained this belief throughout Japan's 2,600-year history.

Today, this ideology perpetuates the present government in Japan despite the continued reverses that the armed forces are suffering. The recent shift in the premiership, and the change in the Japanese cabinet, while indicating disagreement among the leaders as to strategy, is not an indication that the people are ready to call it quits by any means. Every act committed by the Imperial Japanese Government is carried out with the supposed backing of Tenno Heika, his Majesty, the Heavenly Ruler. To know the genesis of this emperor worship is to understand the fanaticism of these people.

Before known history, the Japanese Creator God Izanazi stood on the Floating Bridge of Heaven (Rainbow), and dipped his jeweled spear into the Pacific. As he removed the spear, the congealed drops fell upon the ocean surface forming what are now the Islands of Japan. (Actually, they were formed by one or more great volcanic eruptions).

Izanzi's bride, Izanami, died giving birth to the God of Fire. Determined to revive his wife, Izanazi went to hell. While there, he became so distressed at what he saw, that he fled. In order to cleanse himself of any sins that still clung to him, he first washed his left eye, and Amaterasu, the Sun Goddess, was born; then his right eye brought forth the Moon God; and cleansing his nose created the storm God Susa-no-o.

The Storm God and the Sun Goddess were jealous of each other. Being a temperamental young lady, Amaterasu went into a cave, thus making all the world dark. The lesser Gods (Kami) pleaded with her to show herself, but she firmly refused. The Kami finally decided to trick her. Many of the rituals of Shintoism are based on this act.

It seems the Kami planted a Sakaki tree with 500 branches, and they decorated it with a rosary of 500 jewels, an eight-handed mirror, and offerings of colored cloth. A great festival then took place in which there was much dancing, singing, and laughter. Amaterasu's curiosity got the best of her. She came out of the cave, and immediately one of the Kami blocked its entrance with a large boulder. Thus the sun has stayed in the open heavens ever since.

Amaterasu's grandchild, called Prince Rice Plenty, was sent to earth to govern Japan. He was accompanied by many Kami who brought the three treasures that have since become the imperial insignia. These are: The sword, the mirror, and the jewel.

Generations of Kami came and passed on. Finally, one of Amaterasu's descendants was given the title of Emperor of Japan. This year was 660 B.C. This first ruler was called Jimmu Tenno. He handed down to the people the divine command, "to bring the eight corners of the world under one Japanese roof." This doctrine has been literally pounded into the Japanese people by the generations of military cliques, to sell them the idea that it is Japan's destiny to rule the world.

We don't believe this fantastic tale, but what is more important, the Japanese do. That is why the Japanese

SECTION THREE

soldier flies like a fanatic until killed, or commits Hari-Kiri flights rather than be taken prisoner. He would lose face with the Emperor, Amaterasu's representative on earth, if captured alive, and could therefore not go to the Japanese heaven. The Japanese have long considered a soldier legally dead if he permits himself to be taken captive alive by an enemy of the Emperor.

Most of the common people of Japan have accepted this "divine" mission of world conquest. After all, they say "Japan has never lost a war in its 2600-year history." Our forces in the Pacific are now doing a very thorough job of making this boast ancient history.

On June 28, 1944, I wrote a commentary on the war as I saw it, entitled "Column Left," beginning it with the sentence, "If this past week is any indication of things to come, Adolf Hitler probably wishes he had stuck to his paper hanging." I wrote about Allied victories throughout Europe on land and in the air with the help of the "powerful Red Army" as well as the Japanese Home Fleet turning tail and running in the Pacific. I closed the article with a political commentary: "Here at home our democracy showed clearly above the struggle of the war. The Republicans meeting in Chicago, were about to select their candidates for President and Vice-President. The Democrats move in next month."

Upon graduating as a navigator, I was put on a train to Lemoore Field in Fresno, California. There, I met the rest of my B-24 crew. It consisted of a pilot, co-pilot, bombardier, engineer, radio operator, two gunners, and myself as navigator. After a brief stay, we were transferred to an Air Force base at Walla Walla, Washington. There we trained as a crew so that we were a well-knit team before eventually going overseas for combat duty

23PL-26 Oct 44- Combat Crew #292 WWAAF. Walla Walla, Wn.

Avoiding the Cascade Mountains & Other Hazards

Having heard about planes hitting the mountains, crashing and killing the crews, I thought to myself, "I'm going to war and risking my life, but I don't want to die in the U.S.!" I did some ground research, checking out the major highways from Walla Walla to Spokane that bypassed the mountain ranges and, instead of flying over the Cascades, charted our routes to follow those highways. I carefully calculated how much fuel we would need for the scheduled flight and made sure we came back with the right amount in the tanks. It was my first navigational challenge!

Near our base was a Naval fighter air field. The Naval pilots loved

SECTION THREE

to buzz our bomber base, flying in at almost tree-top level. One day we decided enough was enough. We loaded toilet paper in the bomb bays of several planes and unloaded them when we were over the center of the Naval base. We picked the wrong day. A top admiral was visiting the base and he filed a formal complaint. Instead of rebuking us, our commanding officer said they got what they deserved.

Not far from Walla Walla was a highly restricted area that we were advised not to fly over. It was in the vicinity of Hanford. We were informed that fighter planes based at nearby Moses Lake were on 24-hour alert and would shoot us down if we strayed over their site. No one knew what was happening there. After the war was over, we learned that heavy water and plutonium were being processed for use in the future development of the atomic bomb.

After completing two months of training as a crew, we were assigned to Hamilton Field in San Francisco. Being at a port of embarkation on the West Coast, we felt we would end up in the Pacific Theatre of Operations to fight the Japanese, but once again, the military was unpredictable. We were put on a train that took seven days to cross the country to the East Coast. Our destination was Camp Kilmer, New Jersey. It was the last stop before going to a port of embarkation for the European Theatre.

The New Amsterdam Voyage to Europe

After a stay of one week in New Jersey we boarded the Dutch cruise ship, the New Amsterdam. I didn't get leave to go home before going overseas because I really wasn't sure we were going until we boarded the ship. My brother, Bob, had joined the Army Signal Corps and had been transferred all over the United States to different bases, but never overseas, so my parents just assumed

that was what would happen with me, too. I made a hurried phone call to tell them I was going, and that was it.

We were joined by a handful of other air crews, and 10,000 members of the infantry. Because of the speed of the ship, we did not join a convoy. We zig-zagged across the Atlantic unescorted. The weather was quite stormy and the ship's captain called that a blessing … the rough water reduced the risk of an attack by a German U-boat. A ship several hours ahead of us had been torpedoed. Our Air Force crew was the only group that showed up regularly for dinner – for some reason, maybe our rigorous flight training, we didn't get seasick like everyone else. I remember I played some chess and read a book, And Then There Were None, by Agatha Christie during our voyage. After about a week, we sailed up the Firth of Clyde in Scotland to the Port of Gourock. From there, we took a train to Kettering, the closest city to the 492nd Bomb Group air base at Harrington.

SECTION FOUR

OSS (Office of Strategic Services)

I've been repeatedly asked, "How did you end up with the 492nd Bomb Group, working for OSS?" My honest response has been, "I haven't the faintest idea." I still wonder myself. It is routine for the military to tell you where they want you to go, without consulting the involved individual. I suppose I can call myself "The Accidental Intelligence Officer," but that OSS assignment was a life-changer for me. They made it clear that only the top navigators were chosen for this hazardous duty because of the night-flying that meant you were literally on your own out there. You really had to know your navigational instruments because the crew was counting on you to get the plane to its destination and back, safely, to the base. It was a big responsibility and an honor to be part of such a team. I learned quickly that there is nothing quite so exhilarating as surviving a mission and knowing that the goal was accomplished.

Harrington, England

The 492nd had been transferred to Harrington, near Kettering in Northampton Shire in March 1944. I arrived later that year. The activities at Harrington were classified as "top secret." As with the Mosquito aircraft, all planes at the base were painted black. When our B-24 bombers took off, either individually or in a group, we often spotted British Royal Air Force (RAF) Lancaster bombers also headed for Germany.

It should be noted that OSS was responsible for all American subversive operations in both the European and Pacific theatres. Much to the surprise of German occupying troops, several C-47 planes actually landed in the Lyon area of France. They unloaded

SECTION FOUR

arms and other useful equipment and personnel. The C-47's then took off before the Germans could reach the landing field. The landings had taken place where the French resistance forces called "the Marquis" controlled the area.

The story of the operations of the 492nd Bomb Group would make a great spy movie, with plenty of suspense and intrigue. The Group was separated from the rest of the Eighth Air force in England. The major operation of the Eighth was daytime bombing and strafing of military targets in both Germany and occupied Western Europe. The RAF carried out similar missions during the night hours, as well as defending England against attacking German aircraft. The 492nd Bomb Group only flew at night.

Most of the planes at Harrington were B-24 Liberators. Other aircraft present were the Douglas A-26 twin engine fighter-bomber, the C-47 Dakota or Sky Train, and of course, the Mosquito. The B-24 served two purposes. It was used for bombing missions as one of the diversionary forces for the RAF. There might be three or four of these groups, numbering 10-15 planes. Each had a target in Germany. All dropped thin pieces of aluminum foil (called chaff, a radar countermeasure) to swamp the screens of German radar so they did not know which was the main bomber stream. That force could number 500 to 1,000 planes. One night our target was Emden. The main bomber force hit the Hamburg area, literally leveling the city.

The other key use of the B-24 involved flights of single planes. Those missions included dropping all types of supplies, and/or spies, to aid the resistance forces operating behind the German lines in Western Europe. The place and time for the rendezvous were often carried by the British Broadcasting System in coded messages.

Some years ago, Allan A. Mitchie wrote in Skyways Magazine, "Casual listeners to BBC newscasts were surprised to hear announcers say, 'Uncle Jean has two shillings in his pocket,' or 'Tell Marie to wear her galoshes.' These were coded signals to some French underground operator, often meaning that a plane would be over a Marquis landing field that night to drop arms and supplies, or perhaps drop saboteurs."

At Harrington, our sleeping quarters consisted of a wooden base covered on top with a tent. During the winter of 1944-45, to keep warm, we had a pot-belly stove. For some reason, the stove's fuel would run out about 4:00 in the morning. Towels hung up at night to dry were frozen solid when we got up. So much for Air Force Officers living in luxury.

"Home Sweet Home" - Harrington

SECTION FOUR

Of the 3,000 officers and ground crew men stationed at Harrington, most had limited knowledge of what was happening. It truly was top-secret. We sometimes joked privately among ourselves, calling the OSS – "OH SO SECRET" – but we all understood the importance of confidentiality. Where other officers could write home and talk about some of their war-time experiences, our letters were highly censored and it was better not to write home at all. I know my family wondered what I was doing, as many of their friends were receiving long letters from their sons and my short letters were few and far between.

The American 492nd Bomber Group delivered arms, ammunition, radio sets, food and sabotage equipment to the undergrounds of Europe. For the Norwegians, we dropped skis and sleighs; for the French Marquis, jeeps, bazookas, mortars, bicycles and tires – made in England but with French trademarks. Called the Scarlet Pimpernels of the air, after the hero of a turn-of-the-century novel who fought tyranny in disguise, we transported hundreds of Allied spies, underground agents, and saboteurs under the very nose of the Gestapo. An agent in the Lyon area sent a message to the Americans at Harrington that in the previous month, his Marquis had killed 1,000 Germans with the arms dropped from the air. On a plain granite memorial near the French village of St. Cyr de Valorges is carved this inscription: "In memory of five American airmen found dead under the debris of their aircraft, shot down in flames at this place April 28, 1944, whose mission was the parachuting of arms to our secret army for the liberation of France and the restoration of our ideal."

First Mission

I corresponded with several friends who were also in the Army Air Force, and prior to leaving on the night of my first mission, the

mail contained a returned letter I had written to a fellow navigator in the Eighth Air Force. Across the front was stamped, "Killed in Action." That was not what I needed just before going into combat.

The first diversionary B-24 bombing mission in which I served as a navigator was the flight that had Emden as our target. It was located on the North German coast. To avoid enemy flak, we flew over the North Sea, then turned South towards our objective. As we approached the target area, the plane suddenly appeared to be lit up with light flashes so bright, one could read a newspaper. I told the pilot that the Germans must have powerful flood lights aimed at the sky. Just then the plane started bouncing. The pilot said, "Those flashes aren't lights, Edwards, you idiot! That's from anti-aircraft fire." That was my first baptism in enemy fire. The bombardier then said we were over the target. We unloaded our bombs and got the hell out of the area as fast as we could. Not all our aircraft that night were so lucky.

On another B-24 flight, we carried a beautiful young French woman. She was a "Joe" (spy - women spies were sometimes called "Joans" or Josephines") to be dropped over a part of German occupied France. She spoke excellent English as well as French. She joked with us before the plane reached the rendezvous point. Then she parachuted into the night air. To this day, I wonder what happened to that brave individual. If the Germans caught her, they would have shot her on the spot.

Live Bombs

On one of the bombing missions, two generators became inoperative while we were still over France. The bombardier, Jose, had already removed the safety pins on the bombs. Jose was able to restore the pins into the bombs about thirty minutes before landing, hoping

SECTION FOUR

they were correctly reconnected. We carried 2 ½ tons of bombs. Despite the possibility of flying in a plane that might explode at any minute, we all had to focus on our respective roles because we were still in danger of being hit by German missiles. As we approached Harrington, the tension mounted, and I remember thinking, "Is this the end?" The entire runway area was cleared of planes and personnel, just in case the bombs exploded upon landing. Under extreme pressure, the pilot landed the plane so smoothly that we hardly knew we were on the runway. We had been afraid to drop the bombs in the English Channel, fearing they might hit a British ship, but the outcome was positive and we were safely back on the ground. It was a flight I've never forgotten.

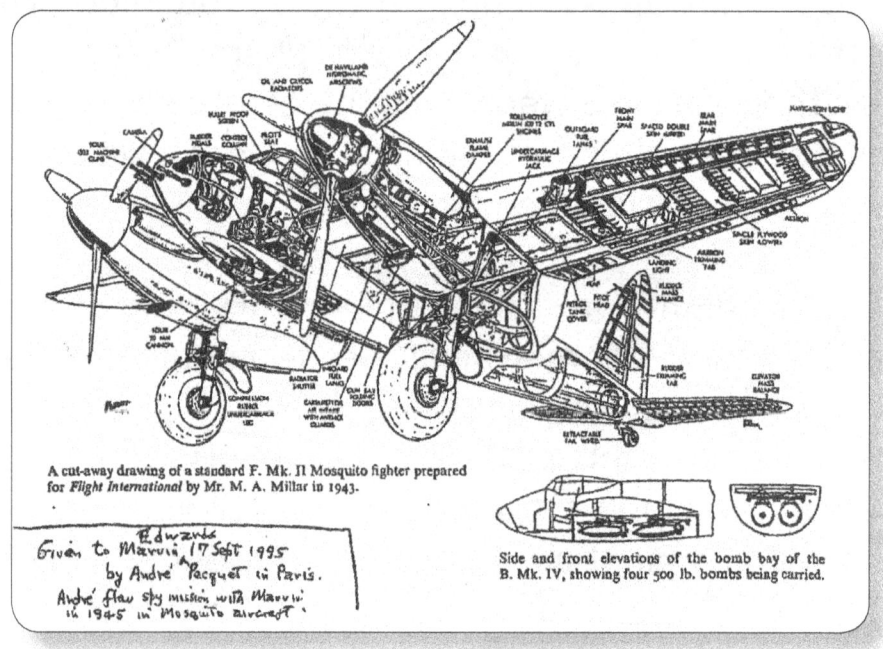

The Mosquito "Mossie"

For a navigator, the Mosquito had many advantages over the B-24. In the B-24, the navigator not only had to wear an oxygen mask, but also a heated suit and heavy gloves. In December the outside temperature at 25,000 feet, the level these bombers flew, could be 50-60 degrees below zero Fahrenheit. The navigator's desk on that plane was located over the nose wheel. There was no air seal, so the temperature where the navigator worked was the same as the outside temperature. Some of the navigational work required removing the gloves, thereby risking frostbite. The B-24 engines roared while the Mosquito engines purred. Oxygen masks were worn in both the B-24 and the Mosquito, but in the engine-heated cockpit of the Mosquito, we were required to wear neither heated suits nor gloves.

Mosquito Crew – Navigator Marvin R. Edwards – front right

Only a handful of American pilots flew in the Mossie. Those that did had some initial problems that required practice to correct. Most American twin engine aircraft had the propellers spinning in opposite directions. On the Mosquito, they rotated in the same direction.

There was one memorable Mosquito mission when a different navigator was assigned to fly but took sick, so I was assigned to take the flight. At the last minute, he reported feeling better and said he could take the flight after all. I was already in the briefing room for flight instructions when I learned that he would be the navigator. Later that evening, I heard that the plane had developed engine trouble and crashed. The escape hatch was located on the navigator's side of the cockpit. Thus, the pilot could not get out until the navigator jumped first. For some unknown reason, the navigator had failed to buckle the chute's leg straps. In order to save the pilot, he jumped anyway. The pilot was saved, but sadly the navigator fell out of his chute to his death. I felt terrible about his death, but took comfort from the knowledge that I religiously went through my checklist before takeoff.

Joan/Eleanor

The sophisticated battery operated radio equipment we used in the Mosquito was called the Joan/Eleanor. The transmission and receiving package weighed about 40 pounds. It could pick up a voice on the ground in the 60-mile width of the cone at 40,000 feet. This transmitter and receiver were called Eleanor. The OSS agent on the ground carried the Joan section. It only weighed about 3 pounds and measured 6.5 inches long x 1.5 inches thick x 2.4 inches wide. While the transmitter used by the agent on the ground spread to a 60-mile circle at 40,000 feet, the cone narrowed to just a couple of feet at ground level. Therefore, the chance of a conversation being picked up by German direction finders was almost nil. The conversations that took place were recorded by the Mosquito special operator on a wire spool.

The small ground transmitter/receiver was designed and built to fit inside a compact suitcase by two Americans. They were Lt. Cdr. Stephen H. Simpson, an RCA research engineer in civilian life, and Mr. DeWitt R. Goddard, another RCA research engineer. "Joan" was

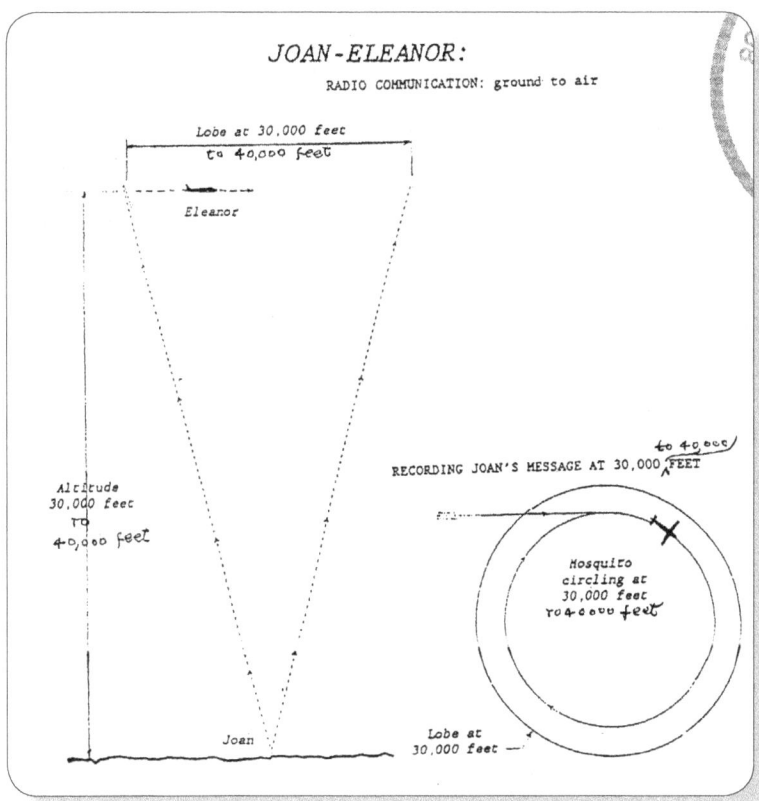

named for WAC Major Joan Marshall, and "Eleanor" for Goddard's wife.

The "Red Stocking" missions, using Joan/Eleanor equipment, as depicted in the Preface of this book and in this chapter as well, were only a small part of the overall OSS operation in Europe. But without it, much of the information obtained by our agents

SECTION FOUR

on the ground in Germany would have been wasted. There was no other way to bring the up-to-date analyses of what the German military was doing, back to the Allied High Command in England.

A couple of "Joes"

OSS Agent Andre Pecquet was one of the most memorable "Joes" who flew several Red Stocking missions with our crew, sitting in the belly of the Mosquito, intent on communicating with the agent below on our Joan/Eleanor radio equipment. Andre wrote a detailed "Red Stocking" Missions report of Joan/Eleanor Training and Operations for OSS, which I kept, of course. I knew it would be important in the future for people to know the intricacies of what we did and how we did it. Excerpts from that report by my good friend, the late OSS Agent Andre Pecquet, are recorded below:

> April 23/24. FARMER-CHAUFFEUR. Flight of 6 hours and 50 mts.
> Pilot LT. KNAPP – Navigator LT. JACKSON
> The first two hours were unpleasant as liquid gas due to some leakage was floating all over my compartment.
> Contact with FARMER in spite of a thorough search was not made.
> Contact with CHAUFFEUR was excellent and lasted 45 mts.

> April 27/28. FARMER-CHAUFFEUR. Flight lasted 7 hrs & 40 mts.
> Same crew as above.
> Gas again leaking all over rear compartment but stopped after an hour.
> Very bad weather. Flew at 32/35,000 ft.

No contact with either team in spite of thorough search over wide area.

May 1. CHAUFFEUR.
    Pilot Lt. KUNTZ – Navigator Lt. EDWARDS.
    Not knowing the exact location of CHAUFFEUR we were to search the MUHLDORF area.
    We took off at 13.45. Compelled to return 40 mts. Later. Interphone, VHF, radio eqpt blew out.
    Tried another plane. Because of several mechanical defects we were unable to take off. The plane was repaired, but while taxiing we discovered that one engine was out of order. By then it was too late for a fourth attempt.

This was my last mission. The surrender of Germany took place a few days later. Flying with KNAPP AND WEBB was of great help as they were aware of the feelings of the operator in the rear, and flew the plane with consideration. They also kept one informed of the progress of the trip.

As in all team work, to fly with a crew you trust is paramount. Should one of the engines fail, in most instances it would be best for the J&E Operator to bail out as being in the rear of the machine, he would have no chance in the event of a crash landing. Flying with a crew the operator trusts, if told to bail out, he knows that the pilot has tried every possible measure and that the best alternative is to jump.

The navigator must be an excellent one who can fly an orbit thus making the difference between a contact

SECTION FOUR

and a miss – or a very poor contact.
To train gradually the J & E Operator is good. Especially in the case of a person who has never flown before under such conditions. Many experienced flyers do not like high-altitude, so for the inexperienced, it is even more important that the training should be by gradual stages: Use of equipment-flying at altitude – flying in the fuselage of the Mosquito.

The Operator
(Andre Pecquet)

Andre Pecquet, for his service during the months of March and April 1945 at Harrington, was awarded the Bronze Star. The Job Description for Lt. Andre Pecquet, signed by Richard Helms (future CIA Chief) on 10 May 1945, was as follows:

Lt. Pecquet is being used as an J/E operator. The qualifications for this job are almost prohibitive inasmuch as the operator must be able to speak fluent French and German, pass a high altitude flying test, and be able to operate the extremely complicated mechanisms which comprise the aircraft and the J/E equipment. He must operate this equipment from a very cramped and dangerous position in the fuselage of a Mosquito aft of the bomb bay. It required a great deal of effort for a non-Communications man to master the operation of this highly complicated gear, particularly under the harassing conditions of high altitude and in a considerably makeshift equipped position in the aircraft. The operator must wear heated and cumbersome clothing as well as oxygen equipment and his position in the tail of the ship is another factor which he must conquer to operate his equipment inasmuch as the tail of a Mosquito is violently

jostled and thrown around in flight.

Lt. Pecquet volunteered for this hazardous work and threw himself into the training whole-heartedly. Although not very mechanically inclined, by concentrated application he mastered the equipment in a short period of time and overcame the first vicissitudes of high altitude flying in record time. He at all times demonstrated outstanding ability, willingness and resourcefulness during his training as well as on subsequent operational flights over his targets.

It should be borne in mind that when the J/E Aircraft approaches its target area, the J/E operator must be in complete control of the aircraft insofar as directing it by means of the directional antennae and keeping it at all times in the proper position for the necessary reception with reference to the ground operator. In order to carry out his functions in the aircraft, as well as setting up SOP's in rigging an aircraft for J/E, the J/E operator must have sufficient rank to make his weight felt with the Air Corps. The Air Corps does not have any knowledge of the equipment or the method of its operation other than what is planned and explained to them by the J/E technicians. It is therefore felt that Lt. Pecquet's high technical training and qualifications would be more beneficially used were he in grade as a Captain for future operations of this nature with the Air Corps.

Andre and I stayed in touch after the war. He and his charming wife, Jacqueline, graciously invited my wife, Helene, and me to dinner at their home in Paris many years later while participating in the 1993 OSS – Carpetbagger Reunion.

SECTION FOUR

**Andre & Jacqueline Pecquet with me at the Hotel deVille – Paris
(Helene took photo)**

Andre passed away in 1997 and we sent a condolence card to his widow, receiving a beautiful response from Jacqueline on February 18, 1997.

Merci de votre sympathie et de votre amitié à André qui m'ont beaucoup touchée.

Il en aurait été heureux, lui qui offrait une amitié et une sincérité sans faille à ses amis.

Merci du fond du coeur.

Jacqueline Pecquet

Another OSS "Joe" was my good friend, U. S. Army Major Rene Deforneaux. We were in the 492nd together in 1944. At that time, he was being dropped into France as an OSS agent working to train and organize members of the French underground. As native of France who grew up in the United States, Rene was uniquely qualified to work with the OSS. In addition to being bilingual, he had an admirable versatility and sense of humor that enabled him to laugh at what would have terrified some other men. For instance, Rene always told the story of being dropped behind enemy lines in unfamiliar French territory, missing the drop spot by six miles, and then, while walking, running into a group of oriental field workers. At first, he recalled thinking he had been dropped in China – "not only the wrong country," he mused, "but the wrong continent!"

RENE DEFOURNEAUX SR.

Rene Julian Defourneaux Sr. died on April 21, 2010, in Indianapolis, Indiana, after a long illness. Born in Lebetain, France, in 1921, he emigrated with his family to New Jersey. At the start of World War II, he joined the U.S. Army and was stationed in London. He was recruited by OSS and parachuted into occupied France to organize and train French Resistance groups. After the liberation of Paris, he was transferred to Southeast Asia with the OSS Deer Team. He parachuted into Japanese-held French Indochina to train a group of natives selected by Ho Chi Minh and Vo Nguyen Giap, who later led the Vietminh forces to victory against the French at Dien Bien Phu.

After World War II, Defourneaux served in the U.S. Army for 20 years before retiring to Indianapolis with his wife, Virginia, and their six children. He was the author of four books. Internment took place at Arlington National Cemetery on June 9, 2010.

OSS Deer Team members pose with Viet Minh leaders Ho Chi Minh and Vo Nguyen Giap during training at Tan Trao in August 1945. Deer Team members standing (l to r) are Rene Defourneaux (second from left), (Ho Chi Minh), Allison Thomas, (Vo Nguyen Giap), Henry Prunier, and Paul Hoagland, far right. Kneeling, left, are Lawrence Vogt and Aaron Squires.

SECTION FOUR

Once his assignment in France came to an end with the liberation of Paris, Rene was sent by the OSS to North Vietnam to assist a group of fighters known as the Vietminh. The American high command in Southeast Asia was impressed with the Vietminh and arranged for members of the OSS to be air-dropped into the area. My friend, Rene, was one of those OSS Agents. Rene later wrote a book, "The Winking Fox," about his experience in Vietnam.

Many years after serving in the OSS with Rene, I wrote an article for Jacksonville's FOLIO Weekly on June 28, 2002, about Vietnam. I wrote about what my friend, retired OSS Operative Rene Defourneaux, had told me about the little-known relationship between the North Vietnamese and the United States. I lamented the fact that, despite dire warnings by many, including France's Charles DeGaulle, we had plunged into an unwinnable war in Vietnam. My article, "From Friend to Enemy", follows:

Washington's Ignorance turned Ho Chi Minh from a U.S. Ally into a Formidable Enemy

In World War II, the French in French Indochina capitulated to the Japanese. Only an organized Vietnamese militia operating in northern Vietnam continued to fight. The American High Command in China heard about these forces, called the Vietminh. These groups had also rescued one of Gen. Claire Chennault's Flying Tigers pilots shot down over Vietnam. The command directed the Office of Strategic Services (OSS) to drop agents in the area where the Vietminh had their headquarters. Those paratroopers were called The Deer Team. One member was Major Rene DeFourneaux. He and I had been members of the 492nd Bomb Group based in England. They were the air-arm of OSS in Europe, where Defourneaux was dropped as a spy in

occupied France before being transferred to Asia.

The Deer Team successfully rendezvoused with a Vietminh force lead by a Mr. Van. Van told the team that their leader was very sick, but he wanted to meet the Americans. The team met a gaunt, sickly individual near death. Paul Hoagland, an OSS medic, diagnosed his illness as malaria and dysentery, and Hoagland treated him, saving his life. OSS gave the Vietminh leader the code name Lucius, but he was known to his followers as Ho Chi Minh. Van turned out to be Gen. Vo Nguyen Giap – the Vietnamese officer who defeated the French at Dien Bien Phu. Giap later created untenable conditions for U.S. forces in Vietnam, resulting in our withdrawal.

Military arms of all types were air-dropped to the Deer Team and the Vietminh. The team trained the Vietminh how to use American weapons, and they taught Ho how to communicate with the U.S. Command in China. Ho kept U.S. forces posted on Japanese troop and ship movements, as well as local weather conditions. This information aided both the Flying Tigers and the American Navy. The Vietminh trained by OSS also carried out skirmishes against the Japanese.

The team asked Ho if there were any favors he wanted. Ho had two: First he wanted to meet Gen. Chennault, which was arranged. Chennault thanked Ho for his help and delivered six 45-caliber pistols for his Vietminh officers. Second, Ho wanted Washington to recognize Vietnam as an independent nation, based on the help they gave in the war against Japan. OSS transmitted the message to both the War Department and the White House, where it was

SECTION FOUR

rejected. The War Department said OSS did not understand the big picture.

Gen. Giap hated the French as much as he disliked the Japanese, and for good reason. Both his wife and infant child died in a French prison, and his sister was guillotined in Saigon. Ho was described by the French as more of a nationalist than a Communist. Ho told The Deer Team that he considered the Americans his friends.

When the Japanese were defeated in August 1945, the Vietminh had a big celebration in Hanoi, where both American and Vietnamese flags were displayed. OSS personnel participated in the event. Then in December 1945, an even larger celebration took place, including a substantial parade. Ho, quoting the American Declaration of Independence, declared Vietnam an independent nation. There was a flyover by an American twin-engine military plane as part of the ceremony. OSS officials sat in the front row of the parade viewing stand and cheered with the Vietnamese. A BBC documentary titled, "Uncle Ho and Uncle Sam," includes pictures of the scene.

French troops again occupied Vietnam in March 1946. During their reoccupation they killed 6,000 Vietnamese. Thus began the Vietminh's 30-year war, starting with the French and ending with the United States. Gen. Charles DeGaulle of France warned President John Kennedy against going into Vietnam under any circumstances. He told Kennedy, in part, "I predict that you will sink step by step into a bottomless military and political quagmire [in Vietnam], however much you spend in men and money."

We saved Ho Chi Minh's life, and he gave us his full support against the Japanese. Then we went all out to crush him and destroy his country. The cost was devastating to families both here and in Vietnam. Unlike the Al Qaeda, which actually invaded the United States on 9/11, the Vietminh were our allies in World War II. It was an American decision to travel halfway around the globe to replace the defeated French in Vietnam. The "Communist Domino theory" did not materialize. From every aspect, the Vietnam tragedy must not be forgotten so it is not repeated.

The formidable fighting force called the Vietminh, led by Ho Chi Minh, were well-trained indeed. They had been taught by OSS operatives like Rene Defourneaux how to use American weapons and communicate with Americans. They knew their friend/enemy well and, as DeGaulle predicted, it was to our great detriment.

At his request, I sent Senator George McGovern a copy of the FOLIO Weekly article I had written about the Vietnam tragedy. I received the following letter from McGovern in response, with the request that I put him in touch with Rene, which I did.

SECTION FOUR

> George McGovern
> 605 Groff Lane
> Stevensville, Montana 59870
> Tel. 406-777-7080
>
> Jan. 4, 2003
>
> Dear Marion,
>
> A belated thank you for your good letter of Oct. 15 and those excellent articles you enclosed. What a tragedy that instead of negotiating with Ho our policy makers sided in with the French colonialists who were doomed to defeat even as we were when we assumed their mantle.
>
> All the best in 2003 — I'm grateful that you and your son were with me in '72.
>
> Sincerely,
> George M.
>
> P.S. Wouldn't it be interesting to talk with Major Rene J. Defourneaux after all these years about his WWII experiences with the Vietminh. Would that be possible? There may be others. I'd be interested in exploring that if you think it feasible.

The "Joes" (both men and women) in the air and on the ground behind the enemy lines everywhere were the real heroes. Their lives were at risk every day. A number were caught, and they were either immediately shot, sent to concentration camps, or died in skirmishes with the enemy. They played an important role in saving the lives of many in our armed forces, and in shortening the war in Europe and the Pacific.

Because the OSS Operations were "top secret," few Americans, even today, are aware of what they accomplished under highly adverse conditions. Now the story can be told. The thousands

of men and women who never returned from these subversive operations should never be forgotten.

London

Harrington was a British Military Base located near London and even during war-time there were light-hearted moments and opportunities to get a pass and go off-base to enjoy cultural pursuits.

Thanks to a letter of introduction from Mayor Alsop of Jacksonville, this time to Viscountess Lady Nancy Astor, I had the opportunity to enjoy a luncheon with her in London at a posh restaurant. Lady Astor later wrote a letter to Mayor Alsop telling him how much she enjoyed meeting me. I believe she enjoyed it because she did all the talking and I was a good listener. She invited me to visit her country estate, Cliveden, and talked about the "Cliveden Set," describing them as a group of political intellectuals. I never was able to make the time to accept her invitation. I didn't know when we met that she was anti-Semitic and she did not know that I was a Jew. I've learned since that she also had anti-Catholic views and that part of her Cliveden

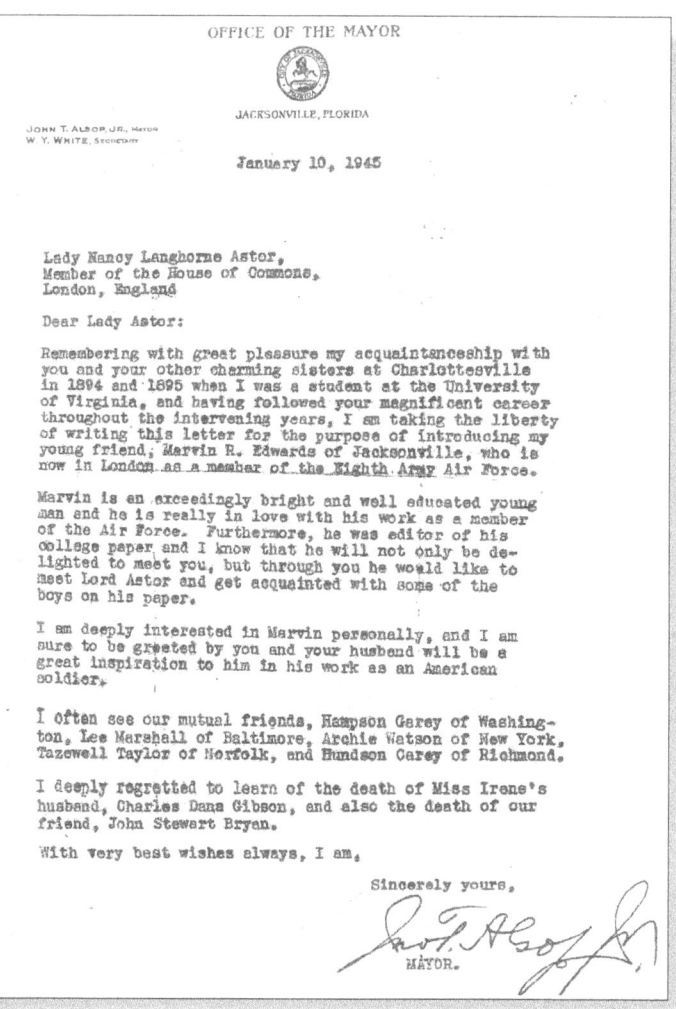

SECTION FOUR

set had even been pro-German at the beginning of the war. Lady Astor was a beautiful woman who was known for her scathing wit. She is said to have had several heated exchanges with Winston Churchill, including a classic one wherein she told Churchill that if he were her husband, she'd poison his tea, and he responded, "Madam, if you were my wife, I'd drink it."

Another Jacksonville connection, this one a personal friend of our family, was Saul Wolfson, one of the brothers who created Jacksonville's Wolfson Children's Hospital. When Saul, who was also overseas serving in the military, heard that I was stationed near London, he contacted me. We had a great lunch at the Universal Restaurant at Denmark Street and Charing Cross Road, where they served English and Continental cuisine. I've kept up my friendship with the Wolfson family for many years and still count them among my treasured friends.

Some of us in the OSS were on a weekend pass to London in January of 1945 and went to the Lyric Theater to see the play, "Love In Idleness" by Terence Rattigan, starring Lynn Fontanne and Alfred Lunt, who were married at the time but not making it public. Although it was billed as a light-hearted comedy, there were necessary war-related notices printed on the playbill that were anything but light-hearted.

Air-Raid Warnings.
If a public air-raid warning is sounded in the course of a performance, the audience will be notified on the illuminated sign in front of the footlights for one minute. This does not necessarily mean that an air raid will take place, and we recommend you to remain in the theatre. If, however, you wish to leave, you are at liberty to do so. All we ask is that, if you feel you must go, you will depart quietly, and, as far

as possible, without disturbing the others. The "Raiders Passed" signal will also be shown on the illuminated sign.

Important Notice.
During "Alerts," no trains run from Piccadilly Circus to Charing Cross, Waterloo, or Elephant; but there are special buses from Haymarket and Jermyn Street. The Booking Hall, Piccadilly Circus Station, is NOT an air raid shelter. If you wish to take shelter, see list in Vestibule.

After reading the playbill, and especially after having experienced a great deal of tense expectation while flying over Germany in the dark, I wasn't really shocked as I sat in the dark theatre, to hear a huge explosion occurring somewhere nearby. The lady sitting next to me leaned over and whispered, quite calmly, "There goes another one." The play came to a momentary halt, but it was almost immediately determined that there was no imminent danger, so we in the audience sat back in our seats and relaxed as the actors went on with their act.

Following a wonderful performance by the Lunts, I went backstage and was directed to their dressing room. I think my military uniform that identified me as an American Air Force Officer may have been the reason I was welcomed so warmly backstage. The Lunts greeted me graciously and we chatted amiably for a couple of hours. I told them that I had felt compelled to meet them because I wanted to congratulate them for their courageous attitude on stage after the explosion and to thank them for being in London during war-time to entertain audiences who so desperately needed a diversion.

Yes, it was war-time, and after tense night flights in the Mosquito and other aircraft, it was time to seek relief from the overwhelming danger we faced and taste another kind of night-life. We attended

SECTION FOUR

dances on base and dated pretty local women, some of them British Officers, getting weekend passes to London when we could. I dated several interesting women and enjoyed getting to know them well. I kept up with some of them after the war.

British and American officers, whether they were married or not, often invited their dates to join them in their tents overnight in order to "keep warm." I, one of the single officers who usually had a steady date, certainly liked to be kept warm on those cold nights, too. We all sought warmth when we could get it because we never knew whether the next flight was going to be our last.

On leave in London during February of 1945, we went to the Palace Theatre on Shaftesbury Avenue to see the Operetta, "Gay Rosalinda" written by Johann Strauss, presented by Tom Arnold and Bernard Delfont. A few days later, at the Prince of Wales Theatre on Coventry Street, I attended a matinee featuring Sid Field in George Black's musical, "Strike It Again!"

There was another restaurant, Maison Prunier on St. James's Street in London, where they served great seafood. I had supper there with some buddies. There was also a Maison Prunier restaurant in Paris, a city of fine restaurants where I later enjoyed several excellent meals, stage plays and performances.

Now that I'm writing this book, I'm grateful that I saved some of the playbills and cards from those by-gone days of dining on English and French cuisine and attending plays where, at any moment, an explosion might occur. The plays and fancy meals were moments of brief escape from the near-death experiences that were almost the norm in our nightly forays over enemy territory.

We lost many friends in the 492nd. Some were shot down. Others were flying too low for a drop to one of the underground resistance forces and crashed into a mountain, killing the entire crew. Some of those on Mosquito missions failed to return to the base. It was a time of courage and sacrifice for all members of the armed forces serving in combat, whether in Europe, Africa or in the Pacific area. It did result in the defeat of Germany and Japan, whose goals seemed to be to divide the world between them.

At the end of the war, I requested a status list of the names of all the soldiers from Harrington to find out about the fate of my friends and fellow officers. Fate works in strange ways. I discovered that there were three flying officers at Harrington with the last name of Edwards. When the war in Europe ended, I was the only one left.

SECTION FOUR

Czech Spies

After the war in Europe ended in May 1945, our crew, excluding the gunners, served the OSS for another four months. We carried out confidential missions that involved flying to numerous cities on the continent. One memorable one was when we disbursed a group of OSS Czech spies in Czechoslovakia so that they could keep an

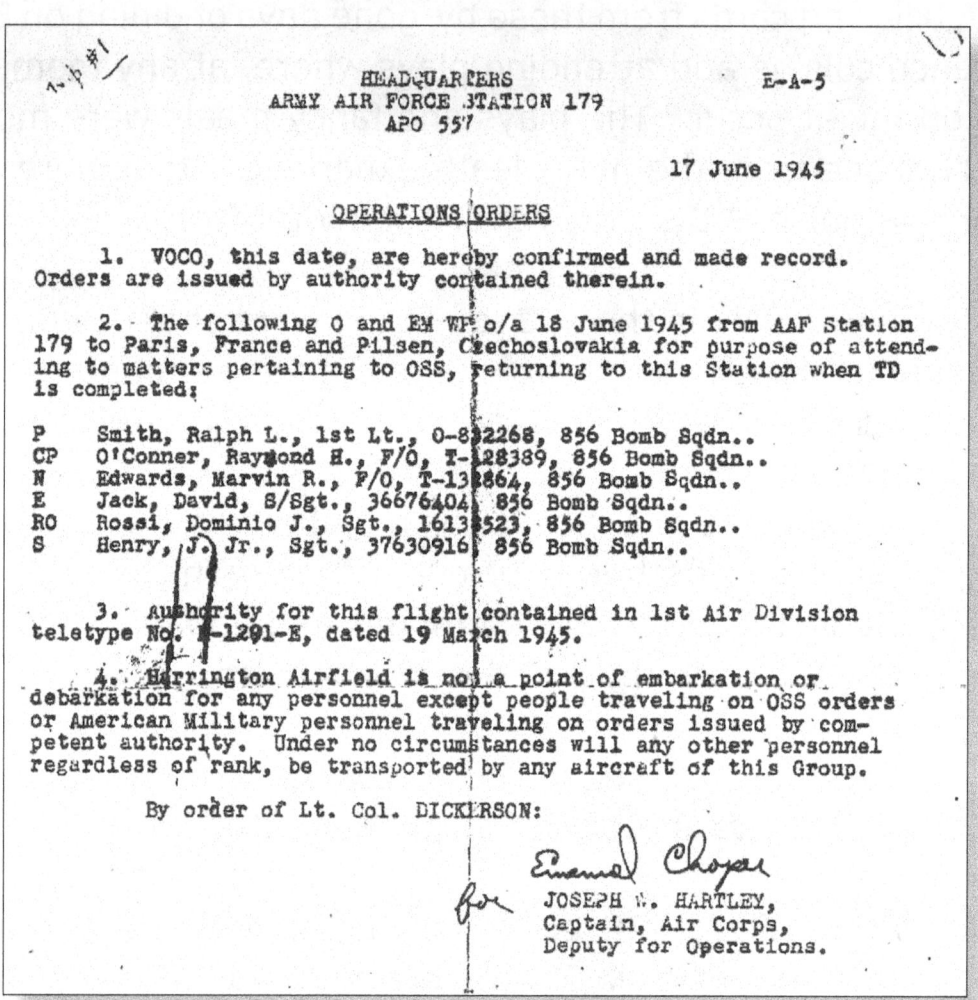

eye on what the Russians were doing in their country and report back to the OSS. Not even officers with the rank of General could fly with us on any of our overseas flights unless they were OSS personnel.

> OSS in Czechoslavakia - A Marvin Edwards photo 1945
> OSS Czech agents in Pilsen, Czechoslavakia after the war to keep the United States posted on what the Soviet Union occupying that country was doing. Marvin was navigator on the aircraft in the photo.
> B-17 Plane

Other OSS assignments followed, as the Orders below indicate:

SECTION FOUR

HEADQUARTERS
ARMY AIR FORCE STATION 179
APO 557

E-A-4.

20 June 1945.

OPERATIONS ORDERS

1. VOCO, this date, are hereby confirmed and made record. Orders are issued by authority contained therein.

2. The following O and EM WP o/a 20 June 1945 from AAF Station 179 to Paris and Weisbaden for purpose of attending to matters pertaining to OSS, returning to this Station when TD is completed:

P	Smith, Ralph L., 1st Lt.	O-832268, 856th Bomb Sqdn.
CP	O'Conner, Raymond H., F/O	T-128389, 856th Bomb Sqdn.
N	Edwards, Marvin R., F/O	T-132864, 856th Bomb Sqdn.
E	Jack, David, S/Sgt.	36676404, 856th Bomb Sqdn.
RO	Rossi, Dominic J., Sgt.	16138523, 856th Bomb Sqdn.
S	Henry, J. Jr., Sgt.	37630916, 856th Bomb Sqdn.

3. Authority for this flight contained in 1st Air Division teletype No. R-1291-E, dated 19 March 1945.

4. Harrington Airfield is not a point of embarkation or debarkation for any personnel except people traveling on OSS orders or American Military personnel traveling on orders issued by competent authority. Under no circumstances will any other personnel, regardless of rank, be transported by any aircraft of this Group.

By order of Lt. Col. DICKERSON:

Joseph W. Hartley
JOSEPH W. HARTLEY,
Capt., Air Corps,
Deputy for Operations.

HEADQUARTERS
ARMY AIR FORCE STATION 179
APO 557

E-A-5

24 June 1945.

OPERATIONS ORDERS

1. VOCO, this date, are hereby confirmed and made record. Orders are issued by authority contained therein.

2. The following O and EM WP o/a 25 June 1945 from AAF Station 179 to Paris, France and Weisbaden, Germany for purpose of attending to matters pertaining to OSS, returning to this Station when TD is completed:

P	Smith, Ralph L., 1st Lt.,	O-832268, 856 Bomb Sqdn..
CP	O'Conner, Raymond H., F/O,	T-128389, 856 Bomb Sqdn..
N	Edwards, Marvin R., F/O,	T-132864, 856 Bomb Sqdn..
E	Jack, David, S/Sgt.,	36676404, 856 Bomb Sqdn..
RO	Rossi, Dominic J., Sgt.,	16138523, 856 Bomb Sqdn..
S	Henry, J. Jr., Sgt.,	37630916, 856 Bomb Sqdn..

3. Authority for this flight contained in 1st Air Division teletype number R-1291-E, dated 19 March 1945.

4. Harrington Airfield is not a point of embarkation or debarkation for any personnel except people traveling on OSS orders or American Military personnel traveling on orders issued by competent authority. Under no circumstances will any other personnel, regardless of rank, be transported by any aircraft of this Group.

By order of Lt. Col. DICKERSON:

Joseph W. Hartley
JOSEPH W. HARTLEY,
Captain, Air Corps,
Deputy for Operations.

HEADQUARTERS
ARMY AIR FORCE STATION 179
APO 557

28 June 1945

OPERATIONS ORDERS

1. VOCO, this date, are hereby confirmed and made record. Orders are issued by authority contained therein.

2. The following O and EM WP o/a 29 June 1945 from AAF Station 179 to Oslo, Norway for purpose of attending to matters pertaining to OSS, returning to this Station when TD is completed:

P   Smith, Ralph L. 1st Lt. O-832268, 856th Bomb Sqdn.
CP O'Conner, Raymond H. F/O T-128389, 856th Bomb Sqdn.
N   Edwards, Marvin R. F/O T-132864, 856th Bomb Sqdn.
E   Jack, David S/Sgt. 36676404, 856th Bomb Sqdn.
RO Rossi, Dominic J. Sgt. 16138523, 856th Bomb Sqdn.
S   Henry, J. Jr. Sgt. 37630916, 856th Bomb Sqdn.

3. Authority for this flight contained in 1st Air Division teletype No. R-1291-E, dated 19 March 1945.

4. Harrington Airfield is not a point of embarkation or debarkation for any people except personnel traveling on OSS orders or American Military personnel traveling on orders issued by competent authority. Under no circumstances will any other personnel regardless of rank, be transported by any aircraft of this Group.

By order of Lt. Col. DICKERSON:

JOSEPH W. HARTLEY,
Capt., Air Corps,
Deputy for Operations.

R_E_S_T_R_I_C_T_E_D   G-A-5

HEADQUARTERS
AAF STATION #468
APO 559

19 July 1945.

SUBJECT: Orders (#10).

TO : All Concerned.

1. The following Officers and Enlisted Men, 331st Bomb Sq, WP by Military Aircraft o/a 20 July 1945 to Copenhagen, Denmark, Oslo, Norway, and other places as necessary on TD for a period of approx six (6) weeks for the purpose of carrying out the instructions of the Commanding General. (Auth: TWX 8th AF D-65368, dtd 18 July 45 and VOCG OSS)

2D LT (1092) WILLIAM A. WINBURN III 0833237   Sgt (748) Frank R. Del Grosso 33731246
2D LT (1034) BERNARD S. VAGNONI   O2069162 Sgt (757) Russell L. Jewett   39918807
2D LT (1092) WILLIAM G. PICKHARDT   0693402   Sgt (612) Franklin D. Stevens   39616979
1ST LT (1092) RALPH L. SMITH   0832068   S/Sgt (748) David Jack   36676404
F/O (1092) RAYMOND H. O'CONNOR   T128389   Sgt (757) Dominic J. Rossi   16138523
F/O (1034) MARVIN R. EDWARDS   T132894   Sgt (612) Joseph Henry, Jr.   37630916

The above Officers and Enlisted Men will be reimbursed for actual and necessary expenses while trav and while at TD Sta where Govt qrs and subs are not avail for a period of approx six (6) weeks and will be reimbursed for actual and necessary expenses. TDN M/A 60-136 P 432-02 A 212/60425. CTRS.

By order of Lt. Colonel MAXWELL:

WILLIS E. SCHWARTZ,
Captain, Air Corps,
Adjutant.

OFFICIAL:

WILLIS E. SCHWARTZ,
Captain, Air Corps,
Adjutant.

SECTION FOUR

Oslo – Still OSS

On the 28th of June 1945, after OSS assignments that took me to Paris, France and Weisbaden, Germany, I was assigned to Oslo, Norway and on June 30th witnessed an "Allied Day" Parade of Russian soldiers marching and singing down the streets of Oslo, thanking the Allies (American, French and British) for rescuing them. There had been approximately 85,000 Russian soldiers who had been slave laborers for the Germans in Norway, and no longer had their clothing, much less uniforms. I found it amazing that about 500 of these Russians marched in the parade due to the fact that there were only that many British uniforms available for them to wear. Seeing this parade really brought it home to me how the Germans had caused the suffering of so many people in so many places. I took several photographs of that highly emotional and historic event.

Russian Soldiers Wearing British Uniforms Marching on "Allied Day" - Oslo

British Sailors – Allied Day Parade – Oslo, Norway

My assignment with OSS following the war came to an abrupt halt on the 2nd of October 1945 with a telephone call from Colonel F. A. V. Hartbrodt, A-3, 8th Air Force, advising the Office of Strategic Services that it would be necessary to recall the two B-17's and their crews who had been working on special projects. I was one of those crew members on assignment in Copenhagen at that time. I was actually staying, by the way, in the Pension Berg

SECTION FOUR

Internationale, the same place the Gestapo had chosen to stay when they occupied Denmark.

Judy Freuchen

Earlier, when I was first assigned in Copenhagen, I stayed in the small private family home of Judy Freuchen, a woman in the Danish Underground whom I had gotten to know through mutual friends in the Royal Air Force. It was a small home and when I discovered that Judy's brother, a doctor, had given me his room, I apologized, saying I would have stayed in a hotel had I known that. I've never forgotten his reply, "Where there is room in the heart, there is room in the home." Many years later, when Judy came to the United States, I reciprocated her family's hospitality by inviting her to stay at my parents' home.

I found myself in Copenhagen so regularly that I acquired the nickname "Santa Claus," because I brought goodies with me – Danish cheeses to England and English Tobacco to Denmark. I was offered a shot of whiskey to trade assignments once in a while, but I informed the others that I preferred "the company of women over whiskey."

Judy and I kept in touch and remained friends long after the war was over and my assignment with OSS was completed, but it was disappointing for me to learn that my time in Copenhagen as an OSS operative had come to an unexpected and sudden conclusion. According to Col. Hartbrodt, under no circumstances, by reason of

the new redeployment order, would the OSS crews be permitted to return to Copenhagen for the completion of the work that was being done.

A letter was written to the Commanding Officer, 94th Bomb Group, by Colonel John A. Bross, Commanding Officer, OSS, regarding this redeployment. The letter stated, among other things, that our crews had been engaged in ferrying of OSS operatives and air freight to forward installations throughout Europe since VE-Day and that all personnel mentioned therein were entitled to return to the United States when the 492nd Bomb Group was redeployed and all volunteered to remain in this theatre in order to continue the operations in which "they had taken great personal interest." He further stated, "It is my desire to commend these men for excellent services to this organization, and to thank them, through you, for their willingness to be of continued service after the disbanding of their former unit, and to express my appreciation to you as their Commanding Officer. The letter ended with the "promise" that the new redeployment program "will return them to the United States immediately." This was a gross misrepresentation, to say the least. I was not returned to the United States immediately.

Rather, in October 1945, I was transferred to the European Air Transport Service, with my headquarters in Munich. At first, I was disappointed not to be returning to the United States, but then discovered that there was an opportunity here to strengthen my journalistic talents as founder and editor of the base newspaper, and also to explore post-war Europe on the ground and in what I thought would be a more peaceful atmosphere. That, I was to discover, was not always the case.

During the ensuing months, I returned to London as often as possible to enjoy stage plays, and on the evening of March 13,

SECTION FOUR

1945, I saw George Black's musical, "Happy and Glorious" at The Palladium Theatre. British Comic Tommy Trinder kept me laughing the entire evening. Sadly, according to recent research, producer George Black died the next day, on March 14, 1945 in London. The cause of his death is not mentioned, however, a BBC Radio tribute was paid to him and his flourishing entertainment empire on April 12, 1945, titled George Black Memories.

Stage plays were exciting and I kept the playbills from several more that I attended in London in late 1945 after the war had officially ended. Thumbing through those playbills now, I see that I went to St. Martin's Theater, where I saw "The Shop at Sly Corner," A thriller in three acts by Edward Percy. "Is Your Honeymoon Really Necessary?" was billed as a "Farcical Comedy by E. Vivian Tidmarsh and played at Duke of York's Theatre, starring Ralph Lynn and Elsie Randolph. The Ambassador's Theatre featured the second edition of "Sweet and Low" titled "Sweeter and Lower" staring Hermione Gingold and Henry Kindall, and at the Apollo Theatre, I saw "Private Lives" a comedy in three acts by Noel Coward, starring Peggy Simpson and John Clements. No more were there Air-Raid Warnings on the programmes, and no more did explosions disturb the actors or audiences. It was a time of post-war celebration – an almost giddy time of relief for people who had suffered war-time depredations and danger.

A musical romance, "Perchance to Dream" starring Ivor Novello, played at The London Hippodrome.

SECTION FIVE

CARRIER COURIER

Soon after being transferred to Munich, I founded a base newspaper, the Carrier Courier. A portion of the following article appeared in the first edition. Considering the state of our world today, these reflections upon Armistice Day more than six decades ago were more prophetic than I could imagine at the time I wrote it.

A Serviceman's Reflections Upon Armistice Day

The most extensive and destructive war that has yet embroiled mankind ended but three months ago. As a member of the United Nations, we contributed a large share of the expended effort that brought about a successful conclusion to that struggle. In our moment of triumph and great rejoicing, we must not forget our obligations to those men and women of many races, colors and religions who paid the supreme price in order that the cause of freedom might live.

Though the tides of war brought the fruits of victory to our shores, the task is far from over. Our greatest responsibility lies ahead. Triumph in battle means absolutely nothing if the cooperative spirit that we became imbued with during the military crisis ended when the last shot was fired. The unconditional surrender of the aggressor states has given the United Nations a chance to put into practice those principles for which their combined peoples fought. Only by a continuation in peace of this united effort to solve all problems of common interest, can we achieve the desired end of good will and brotherhood among all men.

SECTION FIVE

On the 1945 Armistice Day just past, we commemorated the 27th anniversary of the truce that brought the First World War to an end, and paved the way for the tragic era just ended. Our parents made two fatal mistakes. The first was when they accepted a pause in hostilities instead of seeing the fight through until they had accomplished the complete destruction of the German armed forces and war industries. It is fortunate that this error is not being repeated. The second mistake came about when that generation became so overjoyed at the end of the struggle that the very cause for which they had fought faded into oblivion. It is not being pessimistic to ask if this same stigma does not exist in the minds of a lot of people today. It can be verified by the fact that many servicemen who have returned to the States after having served extended tours overseas, have expressed anxiety over the disinterested attitude of many people in all sections of the country. This despite the infamous experience of December 7, 1941, and more recently the advent to the realm of practical weapons of the rocket and the atomic bomb.

If we still fail to recognize and accept the worldly outlook that was literally thrust upon us, then we are not only writing the final chapter to our own history, but also to that of the rest of the world. There will never be another opportunity for us even to think about remaining neutral, or isolating ourselves in a world where any nation, or group of nations, is permitted to commit acts of aggression against a neighboring state. Japan is as much our next door neighbor as Canada or Mexico.

Aggression could always be compared to a malignant growth. If it were not immediately isolated, and then destroyed, it

would spread in all directions, devouring everything in its path. In the future, however, a power bent on subjugating a nation thousands of miles away, would not have to seize nearby territory to gain advance bases. The first warning received by the victim would come when his industrial centers, such as the Detroit, San Francisco, or New York areas, completely vanished under a 60,000-foot cloud of dust and smoke. What once were great cities, containing vast buildings and millions of people, would be nothing but ash. This obliteration would be brought about by rockets traveling at speeds of 10,000 miles an hour, carrying an atomic or cosmic charge, and directed to the pinpoint targets by radar.

It would truly make a mockery of the dead in this and the last war, if we did not activate the words of our leaders in their avowed intentions to have America lead the world into an era of internationalism. An era in which peace-loving states, backed up by their combined military might, would thwart any potential disturber of their security even before he began.

When we have backed up our declared aims with deeds, then, and only then, will the other nations of the world know that America is no longer a wallflower in the community of nations. Then will the chance for a lasting peace become more than just the words of an idealist.

                F/O Marvin R. Edwards
                European Theatre of Operations

SECTION FIVE

The first edition of the Carrier Courier appeared on November 29, 1945.

Volume I, Number 1 — Munich, Germany — 29th November 1945

is published once a week by the military personnel of the 442nd Troop Carrier Group, Munich, Germany. Distribution will be on Thursday.

Commanding Officer
LT. COL. PAUL A. JONES

Editor .... F/O MARVIN R. EDWARDS
Staff Writers .... SGT. LEONHARD PRIMER
SGT. HAROLD GROFEBERT
CPL. SAMUEL LAMBERT

Statement of Policy

To comply with one of the unwritten laws of journalism, we herewith present in this first issue of the Carrier Courier, a statement of policy.

1. The Carrier Courier is written to suit the tastes of the military personnel of the 442nd Troop Carrier Group. When possible, we shall change the contents of the paper in compliance with the criticisms and suggestions that the editorial staff receives from You, the reader.

2. The Carrier Courier will contain schedules of the week's religious services, the movies, sports events, dances, and any other activities of pertinent interest on the base, and in the Munich area.

3. The Carrier Courier will contain as much news about the officers and men in each squadron as space allows. All that we ask is that you turn the news in to your squadron correspondent or direct to the newspaper office (basement of the Terminal Building). The squadron column shall be called "Big Wheels and Spokes."

4. The Carrier Courier will print a weekly "Sounding Off" column. Its purpose will be to stimulate the flow of ideas and suggestions among the military personnel, to help make this the best base under the EAST Command. Questions on subjects relating to the 442nd Troop Carrier Group will be printed with official answers. Start writing those letters.

5. All news items shall consist of facts only. Rumors will not be mentioned in the paper, except in the "Sounding Off" column, and the "Big Wheels and Spokes" column. Rumors will always be labeled as such.

Food for Thought

The most destructive war that has yet embroiled mankind ended less than three months ago. As a member of the United Nations, we contributed a large share of the expended effort that brought about a successful conclusion to that struggle. Triumph in battle means absolutely nothing if the cooperative spirit that we became imbued with during the military crisis, ended when the last shot was fired. The unconditional surrender of the aggressor states has given the United Nations a chance to put into practice those principles for which their combined peoples fought for. Only by a continuation in peace of this united effort can we achieve the desired end of good will and brotherhood among men.

If we still fail to accept the worldly outlook that was literally thrust upon us, then we are not only writing the final chapter to our own history, but also to that of the rest of the world. There will never again be an opportunity for us to even think about remaining neutral, or isolating ourselves in a world where any nation, or group of nations, is permitted to commit acts of aggression against a neighboring state.

It would truly make a mockery of the dead of this, and the last war, if we did not activate the words of our leaders in their avowed intentions to have America lead the world into an era of international cooperation. An era in which peace loving states, backed up by their combined military might, would thwart any potential disturber of their security, even before he could strike a blow.

When we have backed up our declared aims with deeds, then, and only then will the other nations of the world know that America is no longer a wall flower in the community of nations. Then will the chances for a lasting peace become more than just the words of an idealist. — M. R. E.

Christmas in Paris

I spent Christmas 1945 in Paris, France at the American Red Cross Lafayette Club on Avenue de L'Opera, the menu including Crushed Pineapple Cocktail, Roast South Dakota Turkey, Sage Dressing – Giblet Gravy, Cranberry Sauce, Candied Sweet Potatoes, Buttered Asparagus, Pickles – Celery, Buttered French Rolls, California Mixed Dried Fruit, Assorted Candy, Brandied Fruit Cake and demi-tasse. I stayed to attend an Opera, Giselle, at the Theatre National De l'Opera. It was a memorable Christmas … my last one wearing the uniform of a U.S. Air Force Flight Officer in Paris … my last one in the European Theatre.

SECTION FIVE

While in Munich, I took full advantage of attending nearly all of the Operas performed at the Bavarian State Opera during its 1945-46 season. These included Shakespeare's A Midsummer Nights' Dream (Felix Mendelssohn), La Bohéme (Giacomo Puccini), Fidelio (Ludwig von Beethoven), Othello (Giuseppe Verdi), Grosses Symphonie-Konzert (Robert Schumann), and Tales of Hoffman (Jaques Ofenbach). My favorite was La Bohéme.

United Nations

As Editor of the Carrier Courier I was privileged to have the opportunity to cover the first United Nations meetings in London in February and March. I had a press pass and I thought, "Here goes nothing," as I blended into General Joseph McNarney's entourage and slipped into the heavily guarded Security Council Meeting. There, I shook hands with many of the dignitaries including Soviet Vice Commissioner for Foreign Affairs Andrey Vyshinski, U.S. Secretary of State James Byrnes and British Foreign Secretary Ernest Bevin.

I wrote a series of articles about the new United Nations Organization for the Carrier Courier. Those articles are in Addendum II at the back of this book, but below is the UN Voting Procedure, which I felt was of prime importance:

Voting Procedure

Just as in the General Assembly, each member of the Security Council has only one vote. All decisions on procedural matters must have an affirmative vote of seven members. One of the most delicate points in the whole charter concerns the voting method on all matters other than those of a procedural nature. In these cases, not only must there be an affirmative vote by seven of the eleven members, but all the permanent members must cast concurring votes. This is the rule which many authorities feel might become a source of embarrassment to the stability of the UNO. Nothing is mentioned in the Charter about what course will be pursued when a permanent member not only fails to agree to the unanimous decision, but refuses to abide by it. Disagreements on the Council thus far have been amicably

SECTION FIVE

settled. It is hoped that such will always be the case. The future peace of the world hinges on it being so.

I also discovered, through writing articles and editing the Carrier Courier, that my life was in danger from some of the locals in Munich who had not quite surrendered and still harbored a great deal of resentment toward Allies. As a result of a couple of death threats, I acquired a 75-pound German Shepherd "bodyguard" named Thunder.

Thunder had been badly abused by Germans and treated well by Americans. He was by my side at all times. If a GI walked by, he would do nothing, but if a German walked by, he would bristle and growl. He could smell the difference between Germans and GI's. We became great friends and I even joked that he was my "able assistant" at the Carrier Courier office. There was a photo taken of me holding the phone up to one of his big ears so that he could better hear the conversation at the other end and respond. I sent him home by American Express and he stayed with my parents for a while, but he was too much for them and they found him a new home. I never saw him again.

I most certainly did need a bodyguard in those days so soon after the end of the war, as they were perilous times for the "victors" – especially outspoken writers and editors. Some of the resentful Germans made no distinction about who they wanted to kill. One deadly trick was devised, where a wire was tied across the road at night at a certain height level, so that if an open jeep drove by, the GI driving it might be decapitated by the wire. We heard about it happening and warnings were immediately sent out that jeeps were no longer to be open at the top when being driven down any German street, night or day.

Obviously, there was still a great deal of resentment on both sides. Hitler had built two fancy structures in Munich in memory of soldiers who had defended him there. Those structures were promptly blown up by U.S. Forces.

Malmedy Massacre Trials/Uncensored Photos

The most dramatic and disturbing assignment I had as editor of the Carrier Courier was covering the Malmedy Massacre Trials.

SECTION FIVE

During the Battle of the Bulge in December 1944, members of the Sixth SS Panzer Army under Gen. Sepp Dietrich murdered hundreds of American prisoners of war and hundreds of civilians. Their orders had been to take no prisoners alive. I will also never forget the sick feeling I had in the pit of my stomach when I first saw the sign at the crematory at Dachau.

> "This area is being retained as a shrine to the 238,000 individuals who were cremated here. Please do not destroy."

The overwhelming feeling that I had as the trial progressed was hate for the Germans. I felt almost physically sick listening to the litany of atrocities. I took with me our photographer, Pfc. Hawks, who took some incredible photographs during the trial. There were photos shown at the trial of many bodies strewn across a snow-covered field and we were asked, if we made them public, to please place a piece of tape over the eyes of the victims so that they could not be identified by loved ones who might see the newspaper.

On the 25th of May, 1946, my article in the Carrier Courier about the trial was published. The photo on the front page showed the six survivors of the 130 odd American Soldiers killed in the Malmedy Massacre, posing in front of the War Crimes Building at Dachau. They were Virgil P. Lary, Kenneth F. Ahrens, Homer D. Ford, Kenneth Kingston, Carl R. Daub and Samuel Dobyns. The article headline read:

Cold Blooded Murder of 700 Unarmed Americans Described in Detail at Malmedy War Crimes Trial
(Medical Personnel Easily Identified by Red Cross Armbands Among Helpless Victims of SS Barbarism in Bulge Battle)

By Marvin R. Edwards

The first week of the Malmedy War Crimes Trial being held at Dachau Concentration Camp is now past history. No longer are the 74 SS defendants the carefree imperturbable group of men who entered the court room for the first session. Evidence against them has reached such proportions that even arrogant General Joseph (Sepp) Dietrich, the most important of the accused, frequently buries his head in his hands. At other times, he closes his eyes, as if trying

German War Criminals – Malmedy Trial
Gen. Sepp Dietrich, front row, #11

SECTION FIVE

to picture his fate. The defendants are charged with the murder of more than 700 American prisoners of war, and at least 100 Belgian non-combatant civilians during the Battle of the Bulge (called the Eifel Offensive by the Germans, because it originated in the vicinity of the Eifel Mountains) in the winter of 1944-45.

Orders Given to Kill POWs

A few days before the command to advance was given, Dietrich, Commander of the 6th SS Panzer Army, issued special orders to his subordinate commanders, each of whom passed them down to all members of his particular unit. Included in these orders were instructions to the effect that, "the offensive would be fought in a ruthless manner, that methods would be employed to spread terror and panic among enemy troops and the enemy civilian population, that the old rules would be cast aside, that humane inhibitions would not be shown, that prisoners of war and civilians would be shot."

Such able SS men as master sergeant Willi Hendel gave instructions to those of lesser rank, that they were to shoot in windows of homes and at anyone who happened to get in front of the sights of their gun barrels; that all prisoners of war were to be killed; and finally that there would be plenty of "rabatz" for everyone. "Rabatz" (plenty of fun) is the SS term for wanton killing.

World-Wide Manhunt Made

In order to find the SS men who were the active participants in the Malmedy murder, a round-the-world search was

made. All the other nations cooperated with the United States Government in its efforts to locate those guilty of the atrocities. The number of men who were suspected of having any connection with the crime was first set at about one thousand. These individuals were interned at a camp in the vicinity of Ludwigsburg. Here a screening of the prisoners was made to determine how many men would be retained for the trial. After a careful study, the number was set at 74. The actual list of accused was much larger than this, but many of the SS men were killed in subsequent battles, while a few still have not been located. The 74 accused were confined at the Internee Prison No. 2 at Schwäbisch Hall. While here they were interrogated singly to find out how much each knew about the Malmedy massacre, and the part he played in it. Black hoods were placed over the prisoner's head while he was being brought into the interrogation room. This was to maintain an air of incognito, and incommunicado among the SS accused.

After the interrogation, many of the prisoners signed statements which have since been introduced in court by the prosecution as evidence. Many of these sworn statements are an admission of guilt in the carrying out of orders to kill all prisoners of war and civilians. Some of the SS officers have admitted receiving and passing on these orders to murder.

SECTION FIVE

Six American Survivors Testify

The week was highlighted by the testimony of six survivors of the massacre of more than 130 American prisoners of war in a field a little south of Malmedy. These six young men, all civilians now, were flown from the States to give the court a first-hand account of the horrible events that took place on 16 December 1944.

The witnesses are: 1st Lt. Virgil P. Lary of Lexington, Kentucky; T/5 Carl R. Daub of Colebrook, Penna; T/5 Kenneth E. Kingston, Allentown, Penna; Sgt. Kenneth Frederich Ahrens, Erie, Penna; and Pfc. Homar D. Ford, Leeton, Mo.

Lt. Lary gave the first description of how he and his buddies were marched to the field while they kept their hands on or over their heads. After all were assembled, he told how one of the SS men stood up in his vehicle and fired two shots into the crowd of Americans. Just before he dove for the ground, he saw a man about 20 feet away double over as a result of one of these shots. Before leaving the stand, Lt. Lary pointed out George Fleps as the man who fired the first bullets into the field.

T/5 Kingston said that he was grazed three times by small arms fire. After the vehicles stopped firing, SS troops walked among the prostrate forms taking personal belongings and shooting any of the wounded that moaned or moved. An SS soldier walked up to him, removed his wrist watch, and then fired two shots at his helmet. The bullets somehow went through the helmet, but missed his head. For almost an hour after the original vehicles (tanks and halftracks) moved on, other vehicles in the column continued to pour machine gun fire and small arms bullets into the field as they moved by. Finally, after the column had gone down the road, the few survivors got up and made a dash for nearby shelters, in case the SS returned.

SECTION FIVE

Sgt. Ahrens was shot in the back while he was hugging the ground for shelter against the murderous machine gun fire. There was moaning and cries of men in pain all around. Finally, the SS foot soldiers came into the field. They silenced the wounded by pistol shots, or by bashing in the victims' head. The man next to Ahrens was moaning until a single shot brought forth one last gasp. One of Ahrens' close friends was a medic, a Cpl. Ralph Indelicato. He was treating some of the wounded when a shot deliberately aimed at him killed him. He wore a large red cross on his arm and there was also one on his helmet. There were a number of other medics also murdered during the same period.

The six survivors had completed their testimony this past Wednesday, and they then left by plane on their trip to the United States.

Bodies in the Snow

Dietrich - an Old Nazi

General Joseph (Sepp) Dietrich has long been one of Adolf Hitler's most faithful followers. He first associated himself with Hitler at the time of the 1923 Putsch in Munich, and he has since followed his Fuehrer's every wish.

Malmedy Massacre Trial – Sepp Dietrich #11

Among the other important defendants are Brig. Gen. Fritz Kraemer, Dietrich's Chief of Staff; Lt. Gen. Hermann Priess, commander of the 1st SS Panzer Division ISSAH (Adolf Hitler); and Col. Joachim Peiper, the youngest colonel in the German army. He is 29.

SECTION FIVE

Degree of Guilt Only Question

There is no question as to the guilt of the accused. It is only a trial involving the degree of the guilt. From the privates to the generals there is one line of reasoning given. They were merely obeying orders from the men above them. Dietrich is blaming Hitler, who is believed dead. In this respect it is similar to the Nuremberg trial.

The Court is headed by Brig. General Joseph T. Dalbey; the prosecution by Lt. Col. Burton F. Ellis; and the defense by Col. Willis M. Everett, Jr.

After my coverage of the Malmedy Massacre at Dachau, which affected me so deeply and permanently, I felt compelled to write a "Suggestion for Orientation of New Personnel" to the Commanding Officer, USAF, Munich. It read as follows:

1. Most of the personnel recently assigned to this station have shown little or no appreciation of the fact that they are here as an occupying force, and not as a liberating one.

2. These replacements do not seem to have any realization of the many crimes perpetrated by the German people.

3. It is suggested that a trip to Dachau Concentration Camp be made a part of the Information and Education course. The attendance should be compulsory, just as it is for the lectures.

4. A small group could go to the Camp each week.

5. The impressions made on such a tour would be much deeper, and more lasting than if a lecture were given on the subject.

My status as a member of the International Press gave me access to photographs that were published in other publications, and some that were never published. Among the photographs I acquired was one of General Dwight D. Eisenhower at Buchenwald Concentration Camp in 1945. Today, there are actually people who believe that the Holocaust never happened. For that reason, and to honor the many millions of human beings who were brutally murdered by the Nazis, I am placing that photo in this book as a stark reminder that the Holocaust can never happen again.

Eisenhower at Buchenwald - 1945

SECTION FIVE

In addition to writing articles of national and international interest, as well as local items for base personnel, editorials, and suggestions for the troops, I also suggested some ironic cartoons for the Carrier Courier and even tried my hand at writing a short story.

Published in the March 9, 1946 edition of The Carrier Courier, a short story by Marvin R. Edwards:

She Stoops to Conquer – A Story Based on Fact

Ray was Nobody's Fool, but then He Met Hilda ...

Ray Johnson was an overseas veteran of six weeks. He had landed at Le Havre after an unexciting ten-day boat trip. Two weeks of processing and then the transfer to the Wiesbaden base. Office experience in the States, and a shortage of trained clerks for the station personnel section brought about his assignment to that department.

Before leaving the U.S. of A., he had heard returning GI's tell interesting stories about the frauleins. Since he was soon to be a member of the occupation force, he listened attentively. There were only a few sour notes in the discussions, and they usually came from veterans wearing the Purple Heart. "Can't blame them for being sore," Ray thought.

Ray went to the Schmidt Keller his second night in Wiesbaden. It had been highly recommended by his more experienced buddies. It was just as they pictured it. Pretty barmaids, good beer, and a five piece German band that could make with the jive just as he had heard so often at home. He had the good fortune to be waited on by Hilda, the most attractive waitress there. Before the Keller had closed for the evening she told him he could see her home.

As the newly made friends walked hand in hand toward her home they had many occasions to laugh at her faltering English, and his poor attempts at using German phrases. With the smoke from two Lucky's permeating the air, the topic of conversation became one of mutual admiration...

On the way back to the field, Ray got to thinking. "I've got what is probably the best deal of all time. Just a rookie, and I'm already set with a good looking gal who really is cute. Her country was against America in the war, but she said that she was never a member of the Nazi party, and anyway, how could a sweet kid like Hilda ever hurt someone. For that matter, most of the Germans seem like a good sort. Hitler must have forced the people into the war. The propaganda they fed us at the POE about the crimes perpetrated by the Germans was probably greatly colored just so we wouldn't be too anxious to fraternize. Hilda is different. I'm certain of that."

To better appreciate Ray's infatuation with Hilda, let's describe the young lady, and then turn the clock back to the days when the spirit of Nazism still existed openly in the minds of some seventy million peace loving Germans.

SECTION FIVE

Appearance can very easily be deceiving. Especially when it is used to guess accurately a young lady's age. Hilda could easily pass herself off as a girl in her twenties. Actually she was only eighteen. What apparently was a full development at an early age was responsible. To go with a fair complexion, she had blonde hair, blue eyes, and a figure that was just a little on the plump side of shapely. Hilda could be classed as an attractive German fraulein.

This robust girl's home was in the health resort city of Wiesbaden, located at the junction of the Rhine and the Main Rivers. She had heard much from her elders about the many travelers who congregated there between the wars. Her own memory on that subject was not too good. A young girl can't be expected to remember much of what she sees, especially if all her time has been spent in becoming proficient in the Nazi ideology.

For the past ten years, life had been easy. Oh yes, there had been school to attend, but when little stress was placed on such subjects as mathematics and chemistry, and the only history that was discussed was the exciting story of the growth of the Fatherland to the position of "protector of little people," it had become quite bearable. It wasn't strange for a healthy German girl to be enthusiastic about the courses in social relations, and the need for children. Hilda liked the idea that she could have intimate relations without having to worry about the old fashioned custom of getting married.

"Our leader expects every healthy girl to help increase the population. While it is the duty of our young men to take their place on the battlefield to die for the Greater

Germany, it is your duty to produce new soldiers to take the place of our fallen heroes." It had been written on the front blackboard in the classroom for all to see and remember. Hilda tingled all over every time that she read it…

Disturbing accounts of the air attacks, day and night, continued to filter into Wiesbaden. Of course the people from the bombed out cities who flocked there to find a new home, probably exaggerated the damage done. Air defenses could not be that weak. Planes flew near Wiesbaden many times, but they were always on their way to another target. Towards the end of 1944, the roar of the enemy planes seemed to reach such proportions that one imagined that they heard them even when they were not in the vicinity. Mainz, just across the Rhine; Frankfurt, northeast; and Darmstadt, southeast of Wiesbaden, all had tasted the relentless blows form the air many times. Wiesbaden, the health center, remained untouched. Perhaps it was a good thing that it had specialized in cure-all waters. There were no important military installations in the city.

The peaceful atmosphere that existed had been perfect for Hilda to give birth to her child. She was almost eighteen when he had been born. The family had expected her to have a hard time, as she was quite young, and it was the firstborn, however, Hilda didn't' find the experience too painful. In fact, she was so pleased with herself that she wouldn't admit that she suffered any pain at all.

There wasn't much to tell about the events leading up to that maternal event. He was a soldier in the tank corps, and was on his last day of leave. They had met at a party that night for the first time. She knew that his first name

SECTION FIVE

was Karl, and that he was 23 years old. They danced for a while, and had a few drinks. At times, he was forceful in his actions, but Hilda respected him for that. The German girl is taught to be subservient to her man. Karl had made no mystery of his intentions for the evening, and she could not find any reason to disagree. As a grownup girl of seventeen at the time, it seemed like a perfect opportunity to put into practice those ideas that had been instilled into her ... Karl left the next morning for the Eastern front ... The baby would never know its father. Upon completion of the nursing period, Hilda had left it at one of the many state controlled homes for parentless babies. The doctor had said the child was in perfect health, and he expressed a hope that Hilda would come again ...

As the year 1945 approached, military traffic began moving through Wiesbaden. The railroad stations and main highways in and around the other cities had been destroyed or badly damaged. It was reported that a warning had been given to Germany that unless the military movements taking place in Wiesbaden stopped, that city was going to be added to the list of places to be destroyed. The traffic increased in January and February. The railroad terminus was unusually busy, and trucks rumbled through the city with troops and equipment day and night ... the inevitable came the last week in February.

A thick layer of clouds blanketed the city that fateful night. Hilda had gone out alone to take a short walk, a habit she acquired after coming out of the hospital. About 9:30 the first alarm sounded. The people went on about their business. They thought it another raid on Frankfurt or some other nearby target. The roar of plane engines continued

to get stronger. Now the flak guns in the city opened up. The planes must be off course to fly over Wiesbaden. From the sound it appeared to be a small force, perhaps 25 to 30 planes … even though the searchlights were playing tag in the heavens, one could not see the aircraft, as they remained above the clouds. Wiesbaden's vacation was over as the first bombs and incendiaries landed in the area of the railroad station. Hilda stood on the street with thousands of others who shook their fists and cursed the enemy who dared hurt their city. The air raid shelters might just as well have not existed for all the use they got that night. There had never been any need for them before.

Only one section of the city had been hit by these bombs, which it later turned out were dropped by a small force of American planes. This area was lighting the sky with a bright yellow flame, showing where the incendiaries had fallen. Within three minutes the worst was over. The planes were gone … why didn't the all clear sound? The answer was soon given, as a thundering noise, the like of which had never been heard by the people of Wiesbaden, seemed to engulf the city. A main force of RAF bombers was over its heart. The people became panic stricken. Hilda imagined that she could see the bomb bay doors opening, and the bombardier releasing the bombs just as the pictures had shown when the German planes were over Rotterdam and Warsaw. It was fun in those days, but now … Hilda stood in a doorway, too weak to move. This must be a nightmare, she thought.

For almost half an hour, thousands of pounds of bombs rained on Wiesbaden. Many people were trapped in the streets. Not a section of the city remained unscathed.

SECTION FIVE

Mixed with the deafening roar of explosions were clusters of incendiaries igniting everything they touched. It was 10:00 at night, but the city was alight with explosions. A bomb landed near the building Hilda was standing in front of. She was thrown to the ground by the force of the concussion, but the reinforced frame doorway that she stood under saved her from all injury save a few minor cuts and bruises on her face, legs and arms. A thick cloud of smoke and dust rose, and for a few minutes it was both choking and blinding. As it abated, it settled on her body, covering her from head to foot. It took a lot of imagination to recognize the prostrate figure as that of the blonde girl who had been standing in the doorway but a few minutes before.

Hilda made no effort to pick herself up. She just stared into the burning night as if hypnotized by the wreckage and fires that were springing up everywhere. People were running in all directions, but there didn't seem to be any forethought in their movements. Hilda's eyes blazed with the hatred that she felt. "Someday we shall have our revenge on these enemies of the Fatherland. Deutschland uber allies."

It was a few weeks after the bombing when Hilda was hired as a barmaid at the Schmidt Keller, one of the largest taverns in the city. It's proprietor, Herr Schmidt, had once been awarded a medal by the Kaiser, and while he was never a member of the party, he was one of the Nazis' staunchest supporters.

The first day Hilda reported for work, Mr. Schmidt gave her some sound advice on how to act when the Americans entered Wiesbaden. "Play up to them as best you can," he began. "Let them think you are an innocent victim yourself

of the acts of the Nazis. It is most important to remember that by having a pleasant smile when our American enemies are around, you are doing more for Germany than if you killed some of them. If we accede to their demands in the beginning, they not only won't apply more restrictions to our movements, but will relax those they have originally intended to enforce. Commercialize on any weakness the Yanks show, but don't anger them to the point that they will take retaliatory measures."

Herr Schmidt saw that Hilda was giving him her undivided attention, so he continued, "Go out with Americans and satisfy them as best you can. Some of the recently discharged soldiers of the Wehrmacht will probably object to German girls going out with the Yanks, but the older generation knows that is the quickest way to make the gullible American forget what he came over here for. A girl such as yourself has all the qualifications to subtly twist a man's opinions to her way of thinking."

Hilda was deeply impressed. A faint smile shown on her face as she thought, "There couldn't be a more pleasant way to serve the Fatherland." The tavern keeper and the barmaid then drank a toast, "For the glory of a Greater Germany which must one day arise out of today's ruins. Heil Hitler..."

"Yes," Ray was saying to his barracks mate. "I've met very few girls as considerate and thoughtful as Hilda. She has no more desire to see Germany try to conquer the world than I have to see America become an aggressor nation. She is just an innocent kid who likes to have a good time. Good night, Harry, and pleasant dreams."

SECTION FIVE

During its short stint, the Carrier Courier evolved into much more than a "camp newspaper." It became obvious very quickly, following our first edition in November of 1945, that the Carrier Courier was widely read throughout the European Theatre. For example, in April of 1946, I received a letter from ETIS (European Theatre Intelligence School), requesting that they be placed on the mailing list for The Carrier Courier. The letter also requested any information we might have relative to newspapers we might have available for the "ETIS NEWS" – a new unit publication of the European Theatre Intelligence School, United States Forces, European Theatre.

Also, having reprinted columns from the New York Herald Tribune, European Edition (Paris) with permission, I received a follow-up letter on 9 August 1946 from the Tribune's General Manager, Kenneth Collins, thanking me for the fine job I did with the Carrier Courier and noting that he read each issue "with interest and pleasure."

When in Paris, I visited the New York Herald Tribune's European office, where I was complimented again by the staff for my work on the Carrier Courier. Kenneth Collins let me know that there was a job available at the Paris office of the Tribune once I left the military, but the job opening would not last long and I needed to make a decision. On reflection, I decided that I needed to finish my college education at NYU, being only a few months from graduation. That decision took me from a career in journalism eventually to a career as an economist, although I always kept my hand in as a researcher, historian and writer, eventually adding activism to that mix. Through submitting editorials and articles to several local publications, I have continued to this day to use my words as weapons for truth, social equity and justice whenever possible.

Back to the Carrier Courier, one of the men on the staff was a great cartoonist and it seemed that whatever I could envision as a cartoon, he could make come to life. The Carrier Courier cartoons, which were meant to be warnings to the GIs that the German women were not to be trusted, had a big following throughout the European Theatre, as did some of my more insightful editorials (which he also reinforced by illustration).

SECTION FIVE

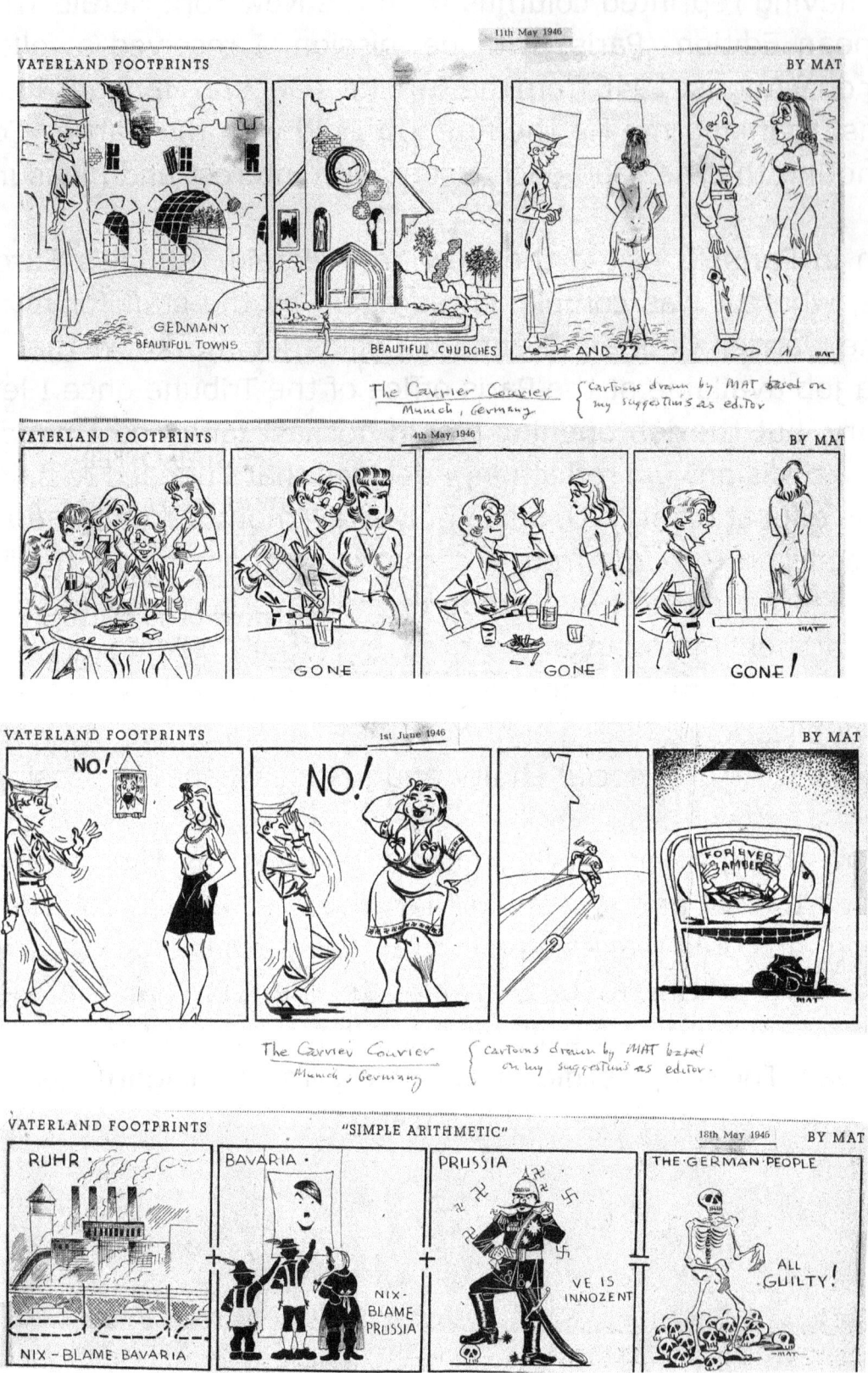

116

An Extravagant Vacation

18th May 1946

Brother, if you came to Europe for a vacation, you needn't look any further. You're in a lazy man's paradise in Bavaria. Just look around you. Beautiful scenery, wild game in nearby woods for the hunter, wonderful rest homes, and beaucoups fräuleins to pass the time with. Just what the doctor ordered———

But wait a moment my fine friend. If you are under the erroneous impression that Uncle Sam sent you to Germany to have a good time, then you had better look about you. Wake up and live.

You are stationed in a country whose people had made it a periodic habit to try to conquer the rest of the world. A lot of your buddies are here for a permanent rest, because they fell while helping to smash the German octopus. They fought to keep it from crushing the world in its tentacles. Is it so hard to realize that the German people you associate with every day were killing your pals just a little over a year ago? The girl who has her lovely arms around your neck today, would have willingly placed a rope around your throat a short time ago. The chances are she would do it now if she could get away with it. She gets more by playing up to your emotions.

There are many reasons for American troops to be stationed here. We have come to help in patrolling this land of international gangsters, to prevent them from striking across other frontiers again. We are here to help reeducate the Germans (of all ages) to make them good citizens of the world. Many Americans have found it easier to listen to the Germans (especially the young females) rather than to try to show them their wrongs, and to change them—American troops are in Germany to show the rest of the world that we will live up to our responsibilities this time, rather than to duck out when we are needed most.

It is important for all of us to remember that we are in Europe as soldiers, not as tourists. It is a responsibility greater than that which rested with the soldier who defeated the German military machine. We must work towards the end that Germany will never again be a threat to the rest of the world.

Just give a few minutes of thought to the idea that our easy and carefree life of today may be responsible for our children's death tomorrow. —M.R.E.

Come Down to Earth Soldier

SECTION FIVE

The Enigma That Is Man

Man proclaims himself to be the great protector of the earth. He believes himself to be the highest type of creature on this sphere. It has always been his reasoning that he should rightfully dominate all other life because of his superiority. Man boasts of the fact that his brain power and ability to think far exceeds these same powers as found in other animals. This slightly haired two-legged mammal achieves the transcendency of self-glorification when he defines his class of beings as the "human" race. He looks upon himself as civilization personified.

It is true that man possesses the greatest brain power, and that he can think much easier than can any other species of life. However, mankind cannot claim the title of the wisest creature on this planet. There are few fights among the other animals as compared with the great number of bloody struggles which mankind always seems to find itself engaged in. Most animals only fight when they need food, or when they want to protect their young. Men start battles just for the sake of conquest and more power. The "human" race is dominated by egotism and greed on the part of individuals, and by overt nationalism and the dreams of having great conquered lands and empires on the part of nations. Man's brain power has helped him to make great strides in the field of natural science, but he has made almost no progress in his understanding of the science of human relationships. This one-sided advancement has been leading "civilization" along the path which will mark its complete destruction. Only by a drastic change in the personality of the individual person can mankinds' future be diverted from its present course towards ruin, to one which is full of hope and great promise.

Six Diseases Man Can't Shake Off

Ever since man first took shape upon this earth, he has periodically succumbed to the influence of one or more of six deadly poisons which plague all who think. These toxins are: Egotism; Jealousy; Greed; Hate; Power; and Conquest. In recent times, the chief carriers of these deadly poisons have been Germany and Japan. Other nations such as Spain have also caught these deadly plagues, and as yet haven't been able to shake them off.

Within the past year, many Americans have come down with attacks of Power and Greed. The diseases have caused these citizens to put

Man's Narrow Vision Is His Undoing

1st June 1946

The Carrier Courier
Munich, Germany

their personal interests far ahead of the needs of their country, and the world at large. The effects are seen by the great number of large-scale strikes which have taken place while the national emergency is still on, and while conditions throughout the world are still in a very precarious position. Management has been misbehaving as well as labor. The attempts by certain management organizations to kill the OPA so that they can obtain greater profits, even though they know that rising prices are dangerous to the country is another example of Greed. A third illustration of this disease can be seen by the way it has caused so many people back home to engage in the blackmarket just because they think they are getting away with something. Unless an anti-toxin is soon found, all of these selfish individuals, whose vision is both narrow and short, will force inflation on the United States. The gains they now make are little as compared to the great losses that would be suffered by all if such a condition were to come about. .

And so these diseases continue to ravage the world. Man seems to be the only creature who suffers almost universally from them. There are anti-toxins that can be used, but no time must be lost in their being injected into the human mind and heart. These cures are Brotherhood; Charity; Goodwill; Love; Justice; and Understanding. They are within the reach of all, but man must inject himself. With the advent of the atomic and cosmic age, time has grown very short. It is ridiculous to speak of improving human relationhips over a period of a few generations. Unless it is done in this generation, we might just as well forget about the future ones. There won't be any. Recognizing this fact, let us make todays' dreams, tomorrow's realities.

—MRE

HEADQUARTERS

USAF STATION MUNICH.

APO 206.U.S.Army.
31 May 1946.

SUBJECT: Commendation.

TO : F/O M.E.Edwards.USAF Station Munich,APO 206.U.S.Army.

1. It is my desire to commend you for your wholehearted devotion to the publication of a superior Station Newspaper. Since its first publication in October 1945 the "Carrier Courier" has without partiality presented the news and activities of USAF Station Munich, and other news of the world in a most interesting manner. Under your Editorialship the "Carrier Courier" has been established in the European Air Transport Service and other Commands as a Model Publication.

PAUL A JONES.
Lt.Col.Air Corps.
COMMANDING.

SECTION FIVE

As my letters home had been heavily censored due to the top secret work I was involved with in the OSS, I wrote much less frequently to my family than I would otherwise have done. It was a relief, once the war was over, to be able to once again write the detailed accounts of events that they had gotten accustomed to from my previous letters home. In January 1946, I wrote a "mock" radio broadcast home to be shared with "Mr. and Mrs. Average American" – the "broadcast" follows:

> January 1946. This is the "Long Ago and Far Away" Broadcasting Company. Station S-N-A-F-U, Munich, Germany. Operating on a frequency of 58 points, S-N-A-F-U is owned by the U.S. Army at present ... your announcer from now until redeployment, which is still a few months off, is F/O Marvin R. Edwards ...
>
> Here is a summary of the latest news, as it was compiled in the S-N-A-F-U newsroom from many and varied sources ... All opinions expressed in this news broadcast are necessarily those of your raving reporter ...
>
> As per custom, here is the latest weather report. Locally, haze, with no sign of clearing ... Washington, and the rest of America ... thick fog, with extremely poor vision ... Bavaria, generally, storms brewing but hard to find their origin ... S-N-A-F-U, Munich.
>
> Before continuing with the remainder of the news, I'd like to wish you dear Mother and Dad (Bob), a very happy New Year. Greetings to Savannah, and please extend my good wishes to all of our friends in Jacksonville, and all the family.
>
> I'm happy to report that I'm in the best of health, and

despite the setback of a few months in my homecoming, my morale is high ... I want to get home as soon as possible, but so do a few hundred thousand other young men ... I've learned patience from the army.

The following exclusive news analysis is addressed to Mr. and Mrs. Average American, and it expresses the feelings of most of the young men overseas.

America fought a war for a good cause in 1917-18, but the people were too short-sighted to realize that the war did not end when the fighting ceased. As a result, they found themselves engulfed in a greater war, with higher stakes, just 25 years later. This second conflict should have convinced even the most blind that we must see the job through this time ... or else!

But once again, the American people have shown their unwillingness to accept the responsibility that is theirs. As soon as the fighting ended, the American people, almost as a single body, demanded that the army be cut to the bone ... "Get all the men home" ... "don't send John overseas, he is too young" ... certainly not Paul, he is too old" ... "Harry has a family" ... "Ted has been in the Army too long in the United States." The results of this talk are: Pressure applied to a politically minded Congress, which brings pressure to the War Department. They in turn begin a large scale redeployment and discharge movement which, because it is rushed, cannot be done efficiently.

So today we find most of the low point men who were to be overseas replacements in civilian clothes ... the drafting of new men has strangely fallen far short of the quota

SECTION FIVE

that was set ... the other United Nations believe we are walking out on them. Our former enemies just laugh at us. The man still overseas has become resentful and feels the people at home have forgotten him. Once again he hears of management fighting for higher profits, and lower taxes; of labor striking for higher wages ... he sees the occupation become a farce because it hasn't the backing of the people at home. He can't understand why there should be shortages of material for the occupation troops. An acute gasoline shortage not only curtails the necessary functions of the occupational army, but in some cases brings them to a complete halt. That is why the man overseas expresses his disgust, and loses any interest he may have had in his job. "Business as Usual" is a very contagious disease, and one which the American people can't seem to shake off. Its deadly bacteria have reached out to the four corners of the globe, wherever American troops can be found. Don't forget, it started within the continental limits of the United States.

The American people were roughly awakened from one deep slumber in December 1941, but now they appear to be falling into another slumber. America has had a golden opportunity to lead the world into an era of understanding and peace. That opportunity is fast becoming a myth, just as it did in the years that followed the end of the First World War.

It is important to remember that THERE IS NO VALOR IN IGNORANCE. The only reward is despair and death.

This is the American people's last chance. We cannot ... we must not throw it away.

****

Mother and Dad (Bob), I ask you to play this record for as many people as possible. I realize that most of the people who hear this record may make a few comments, and that will be the end of it. But if only one person out of all who have heard this record has the courage to exercise some of the freedoms that he or she has been granted under our constitution and writes a letter to his congressman, newspaper, or both, I will feel this record has accomplished its purpose.

****

In case you have done any worrying about me, please don't anymore. Though the newspaper keeps me quite busy, it is work I enjoy. Time is passing very quickly, and before you know it I'll be home. Take care of yourselves and keep well.

Lots of love and kisses, Marvin.

P.S. If you like this record, I'll make some more in the near future. They will not be so serious ... this is the first record that I've made in about five years. The last one was at NYU for a speech course. Munich is now digging itself out of almost two feet of snow ... that is all for now. This is station S-N-A-F-U signing off...

Here is a letter I wrote from Berlin, Germany on April 17, 1946 – Wednesday evening:

Dear Folks,

Another capital city has been added to those that I've visited ... First was Washington DC, then London, followed by Paris,

SECTION FIVE

Copenhagen, Oslo, then Stockholm last month, and now Berlin ...

The basketball team went up here theoretically to play a game, and I went along to write it up, and to get flying time ... There was no game ... I left Munich Tuesday morning by plane ... Flew to Frankfurt, but did not land there. Just called in that we were over the field and then proceeded to Berlin. Whole trip took 2 ½ hours. Munich is 75 percent destroyed, but Berlin is about 85 percent knocked out. Spent yesterday afternoon with "Red" O'Connor ... am living in his apartment which he has at Tempelhof Air Field. He lives with two other boys in four rooms. The airfield is the largest and most beautiful that I've ever seen. It was strafed, but never bombed, surprising as it may seem. Many of the buildings are burned out thanks to the Russians. It is said that when the "Red" troops heard that they couldn't keep Tempelhof, they decided that we couldn't get the place in almost perfect condition, so they used flame throwers and burned up everything they could. It is true that the Germans held out for a while in some of the airfield buildings, but not in all the ones that are burned out.

After supper went with Red and some other officers to a night club called Adra-Gaststattenbetrieve – Stage show, and dancing ... I was the only one who didn't pick up a fraulein. Had taken a ride through the American zone in the afternoon on Tuesday ... Tempelhof was never really finished ... work stopped on it in 1942.

Got hold of a jeep and German driver this afternoon, and went on a sight-seeing tour of the city ... went with two of the other officers who came up with me. Went through the

English, French and Russian zones ... it was another one of those experiences that I'll never forget, as is this whole trip. I'll list some of the places that I saw, and the condition that they are in ... Air Ministry (pretty good, but this is probably due to the fact that the walls are thick concrete); Propaganda Ministry (rubble); Reichschancellery (rubble); Nazi Party Building (rubble); President's Palace (rubble); Kaiser Wilhelm's Palace (fair); Berlin Opera House (Very poor); National Art Gallery (poor); Cathedral of Berlin (poor); Alexander Platz and surrounding area (rubble); Berlin City Hall (poor); Arsenal Museum (very poor); Monument of Unknown Soldier (poor); University of Berlin (very poor); Brandenburg Gate (fair); Reichstag Building (very poor); Olympic Stadium (good) ... By "rubble" I mean there is no building left; by "very poor" I mean just some walls standing which give an idea of what the building looked like; by "poor" I mean a building that is almost destroyed, but still has certain parts of the inside left; by "fair" I mean a building that might be repaired. I went through the Olympic Stadium (built for the 1936 Olympics). It was only damaged a little by shell fire ... can seat about 100,000 I believe. Drove around the Spree River, the Tiergarten (once full of trees, but now just dirt); and Unter Den Linden ... I did not see one building in all of my travels around Berlin that did not have some war scars, whether by bomb (most of the damage), shell, bullet or flame thrower. There are still unrecovered bodies in the city... a concrete building. They decided to hold out against the Reds. The Russians lined the street with tanks and cannon, plus flame throwers, and just fired round after round into the building. There is nothing left but a pile of rubble. No prisoners were taken.

The Americans and English do not carry guns, except the military police. All the Russians carry pistols or rifles, and in

SECTION FIVE

many cases both. Some carry machine guns.

<u>… I am sorry to say that all is not well with the United Nations. Many stories have come out of Berlin, Vienna, and other areas where the Reds and Americans or English mixed. It was my intention to keep an open mind until I saw for myself … I have now, and frankly, the situation "stinks." Russia is playing a lone and forceful hand … unless we have a showdown now as to her actual intentions, there is going to be great trouble in the future. It is not the Russian peoples' fault, but they must take the blame for the acts of their government. The mistake that I have long believed might cause the worst trouble was the dividing of Germany into separate zones. If the United Nations (especially England, America and Russia) can't occupy Germany jointly instead of separately, they might just as well fold up now. All the friction that now exists would have to clear up if the Americans and Russians had to work side by side. There would be no chance for rumors to spring up over Russia's secrecy.*</u>

There are other items I could mention, but will wait until some future date. I went to an early movie this evening – did not do anything else. "Red" flew to Paris today. Expects to be back tomorrow. I'm leaving Friday morning. That is all for now. Will mail rest of money orders when I get back to Munich. Need ten hours flying time this month. Then I will stop my flying. Have three months' pay coming the first of May … will send all home. It will either be about $500 or $700 depending on my flying time.

That is all for now … Lots of love and kisses, Marvin

P.S. "Thunder" is staying with another officer until I return…

*Prophetic

SECTION SIX
BACK IN THE USA

Back to NYU

I had three months left to complete my degree at NYU, so I went to stay with my father's brother, Edwin Edwards, and his family, only a short walk to the 8th Avenue Subway, which I took to NYU. While there, I wrote a few essays and the following one gives you a glimpse into the state of my mind after I returned from the European Theatre. The stark contrast between my remembered view of the Airfield at Pilsen and that of the New York that was beyond my window is evident in excerpts of this essay, written during my last three months at NYU:

Descriptions of This Place, That Place, and Every Place ... Here, There, and Everywhere ... As They Appeared to Me...

Airfield at Pilsen, Czechoslavakia in June 1945

The airstrip is a pasture just long enough to permit planes to land on it. The grass on the field rises in certain sections to a height of two feet. Skeleton remains of the only hangar stand out on the south side of the field. Bomb and shell craters have plastered a great part of the area. The holes have been filled in on the runway.

Many wrecked German planes lie about. These retired bombers and fighters present an ominous background. Some of the aircraft are resting flat on their bellies. Others have their wings planted in the ground. A few can be seen standing on their respective noses, with wings, displaying

SECTION SIX

German crosses, spread out as if trying to balance the plane's precarious position. The greater number of the planes, however, are just piles of junk.

About a hundred Czech men, women and children are walking about in the field. Most of them have no shoes or stockings, and what little clothes they wear is nothing more than rags. The men and boys have on patched blouses and pants. The girls and women have plain dresses on, with the skirts well above their knees. Most of the people look undernourished. They have thin, long legs and frail bodies. The complexion of these citizens is tan, and their hair ranges from blonde to brown. These people are trying to salvage the few useful items left on the field.

****

Looking out of my window, which faces due east on 79th Street and Columbus Avenue, one has an excellent view. My room is on the fifteenth floor. Almost directly in front of me stands the impressive and sprawling massive structures of the Museum of Natural History. The buildings extend from 77th Street to 81st Street, north and south, and from Columbus Avenue to Central Park West. Most of the buildings, which are from five to eight floors in height, are made of various shades of red brick.

The oldest buildings in the group are located on the 77th Street side. The roofs are of a bright red brick, and the walls are of a stone that has a dull dirty red color. The buildings look somewhat like fortresses, because of the massive form that they have, and because of the stone walls.

The structures on the 81st Street side are relatively new. They are all red brick construction. On the Columbus side at 79th Street is the power plant of the Museum. From a stack about eight floors high, steam gushes out constantly. On a damp day, the steam almost acts as a perfect smoke screen, blocking out most of the view.

The newest building is located on the 81st Street side, just off Central Park West. This is the Hayden Planetarium which has a red brick base, and a copper dome that has turned green. When a performance is given at night, powerful searchlights light up the dome.

As the buildings are set quite far back from the streets, a park has been built around them. It is called Museum Park and is a very popular center when the weather is nice. Many mothers and nurses take their children there to play. Benches line the area on the 81st Street side. In the summer, some of the older men of the local community bring chess and checker games to the park. They can be seen playing during the day, and at night under lamp posts. Interested spectators crowd around to watch.

From fall until the new grass seeding in the spring, many football games are played on the lawn. After the new seeding, "Keep off the grass" signs are posted all over. The neighborhood dogs ignore the signs and go where they want all year round.

Looking over the top of the Museum area, Central Park is visible. Behind this open space is the skyline of East Manhattan beginning at 5th Avenue. Just in front of the skyline, across from the Museum of Natural History, is the

SECTION SIX

Museum of Art located in Central Park off 5th Avenue. This Museum is not as large as the one already described, but it is similar in structure, and color, with the exception that the two extreme buildings (north and south) are tan in color.

After graduating from New York University's School of Commerce, Accounts and Finance with a B.S. Degree, I moved to Jacksonville, Florida to be near my family.

Move to Jacksonville

My brother Bob had gotten out of the Army and already had a successful industrial supply business in Jacksonville when I arrived. For a while, I did some freelancing for several local publications and then, in addition to my extra-curricular activity of writing, I opened my own supply business, White Star Sales Corporation in late 1947.

Soon after returning home to Jacksonville, I submitted an article to the Jacksonville Journal regarding the Malmedy Massacre Trials that I had covered at Dachau and written about extensively in the Carrier Courier. The article ran on Friday, July 12, 1946. There was a little box within the article featuring a headshot of me and explaining that I had covered the trial for a military newspaper. It read:

Marvin R. Edwards, son of Mr. and Mrs. Albert H. Edwards, River Oaks Road, returned to Jacksonville last week after three and a half years in the service, 20 months of which was in the ETO. Ranking as a flight officer and stationed at Munich Air Base, Edwards covered the beginning of the Malmedy trial as editor of the base newspaper. With the Eighth Air Force, Edwards worked with the underground

organizations in France, Norway and Denmark. He covered the United Nations conference in London and wrote a series of articles on the conference for the Carrier Courier, the Munich USAF paper.

Excerpts from that article, with the headline, follow:

Jaxon Who Saw Malmedy Trial Tells How SS Men Wilted Under Mass of Evidence
By Marvin R. Edwards

The Malmedy war crimes trial, held in the confines of the notorious Dachau concentration camp is now over. Only the sentencing of the 73 SS defendants found guilty still remains to be done.

To those of us who attended the trial, the verdict just handed down by the seven-man military court, headed by Brig. Gen. Dalbey, had become a certainty even before the prosecution had finished its case. When the trial began in late May, the evidence had accumulated so rapidly against the accused that there was no longer any question of their guilt. From then on, the only detail remaining for the court to carry out was to determine the actual degree of guilt of each of the defendants.

Much of the remainder of the article was reflective of the article that ran in the Carrier Courier. The article also included a couple of the original photos taken at the scene of the Malmedy Massacre, and it ended with the following two hopeful paragraphs, written prior to the final sentencing of the Nazi war criminals:

SECTION SIX

> It had been the hope of the prosecution lawyers to send all of the men to the gallows. They reasoned that when men engage in wanton murder with the idea of making sport out of it, they would make a mockery of justice by being given any lighter sentence.
>
> The German people are watching the results of these trials with great interest. Not because they have any love for justice, but because they want to see how stiff a penalty will be meted out to violators of international law. The next week will tell the story, when the court passes sentence on the accused.

Sadly, the final results of the trials were far from stiff and the lighter sentences meted out were most certainly a mockery of justice. Having experienced the trial first-hand, seen the demeanor of the accused and heard the testimony of the victims, it shocked me that many of these wanton murderers were barely punished. One of the reasons for the light sentences was that certain politicians pleaded for leniency for these Nazi criminals, including the infamous Senator Joseph McCarthy. The worst of the lot, General Sepp Dietrich, ended up serving less than 10 years in prison. The New York Times notice of his death, below, tells the sad tale of misplaced justice for one of Hitler's most maniacal generals.

One paragraph of the New York Times article on Dietrich's death, dated Aril 23, 1966, states, "On Dec. 17 a unit of Dietrich's troops led more than 100 American prisoners into a field near Malmedy, Belgium, and gunned them down with two machine guns. Survivors later testified they heard 'maniacal laughter' during the three minutes of gunfire." And it was the leader of this horrible massacre that had his life sentence reduced to 25 years (and only served ten of them) due to the intercession of Senator Joseph McCarthy, a

man who, in my opinion, shared many of the brutal, inhumane and insensitive characteristics exhibited by the German General.

SATURDAY, APRIL 23, 1966.

SEPP DIETRICH, 74, A HITLER GENERAL

Bodyguard Chief Jailed Till '55 for War Crimes Dies

NEW YORK TIMES

STUTTGART, Germany, April 22 (UPI)—Sepp Dietrich, chief of Adolf Hitler's bodyguard and commander of the troops who massacred more than 100 American prisoners at Malmedy, Belgium, in 1944, died of a heart attack today at his home in Ludwigsburg. He was 74 years old.

Dietrich, who after World World War II was convicted of war crimes and served almost 10 years of a 25-year prison sentence, is survived by his widow and three sons. He had lived apart from his family in his last years.

A Ruthless Follower

Dietrich was known as one of Hitler's most fanatical and ruthless followers. He first met the future Fuhrer during his years of right-wing agitation in Bavaria in the early 1920's, and he quickly became one of his strong-arm men.

A native of Bavaria, Dietrich had worked as a farm hand in his early years. Bored with the rural life, the rugged youth became a professional soldier in 1911 and during World War I fought on the Western and Italian fronts.

After the war he was appointed to the Munich police department. Hitler was then recruiting embittered army veterans for the German Workers party, later renamed the National Socialist German Workers, or Nazi, party, and Dietrich was spell-bound along with thousands of others.

When Hitler launched his premature bid for power in a Munich beer hall in November of 1923, Dietrich was there.

Convicted in Rohm Massacre

Following the failure of the attempted putsch, he remained with Hitler and rose through the ranks of the S.S., the black-uniformed Nazi organization that was rivaling the then more powerful S. A., Hitler's Brown Shirts. In 1957 he was convicted of complicit in the massacre in 1934 of Ernst Rohm, chief of the Brown Shirts, and about 1,000 of Rohm's men.

During the 1930's Dietrich took command of Hitler's bodyguard regiment, and he was called "the man most directly responsible for Hitler's life."

In World War II he joined the Waffen S. S., the Elite Guard of the German armed forces that wa patterned after the original S. SV. As the war turned against the Nazi Hitler put the faithful Dietrich in command of the Sixth S.S. Panzer Army. In August of 1944 he was reported to be heading that unit in Normandy when he was promoted to colonel general one of the top ranks in the S.S.

Leader in Battle of the Bulge

In December of 1944, Dietrich led the Sixth Panzer Army in the famous Ardennes offensive that sought to break through Allied lines to Antwerp. The resulting Battle of the Bulge was one of the Nazi's final lunges.

On Dec. 17 a unit of Dietrich's troops led more than 100 American prisoners into a field near Malmedy, Belgium, and gunned them own with two machine guns. Survivors later testified they heard "maniacal laughter" during the three minutes of gunfire.

A reporter who accompanied the United States Third Army during the battle recalls that when the American troops came upon the field several days later they saw many "snow-covered mounds." The soldiers cleared the snow with brooms and discovered the bodies of the prisoners.

Dietrich led the Sixth Panzer Army to defeat by the Soviet army at Lienna in April, 1945. In the final days of the way he accompanied Clara Petacci, mistress of Benito Mussolini, on her journey to the Italian dictator's mountain retreat.

Cited Hitler's Orders

In 1946 Dietrich was tried with 73 others for the Malmedy massacre by a nine-man United States military court sitting in Dachau. He testified that Hitler had ordered the executions, saying, "The Fuhrer said we would have to act with brutality and show no humane inhibitions."

Dietrich was sentenced to life imprisonment, but the sentence was later reduced to 25 years. He was released in October of 1955 after serving almost 10 years in the Landsberg prison in Upper Bavaria.

NEW YORK TIMES, S

Sepp Dietrich
Associated Press

SECTION SIX

Just as there is no Statute of Limitation on murder, there is no Statute of Limitation on memory either. I have never forgotten the echoes of terror I heard in my heart at every turn in Dachau Concentration Camp, the faces of the perpetrators and victims at the Malmedy Massacre Trial that occurred at Dachau, and the fact that not one of the 74 murderers went to the gallows because Senator Joseph McCarthy interceded on their behalf. The stark photographs of dead bodies of American soldiers in the snow remain in my mind's eye to this day. So, it amazed me to read an editorial in the Florida Times Union newspaper in 1998 that supported McCarthyism and attempted to excuse Senator McCarthy of guilt for the incredible damage he caused to so many during his storied career.

On September 22, 1998, I wrote an article for my column, The Paper Trail, which ran in FOLIO Weekly regularly. My article, titled "RIGHT FROM WRONG, Attempts to reinvent Sen. Joe McCarthy Ignore His History of Evil", follows:

> Remember Joseph McCarthy, the Wisconsin senator whose anti-communist crusade ruined thousands of lives in the 1950s? Historians almost universally regard McCarthy as one of the true scoundrels of modern American history – an evil man whose congressional witch hunt threatened the foundation of our republic.
>
> Forty years later, most Americans draw a blank when McCarthy's name is mentioned. Thus, in many ways, the time is ripe for his reinvention. Witness a recent Florida Times-Union editorial.
>
> The editorial indicated support for McCarthy's "red-baiting" excesses and attacks on individuals who were critical of what became known as McCarthyism.

"For all the zeal Senator Joe McCarthy put into his 1950s anti-communism crusade, the backlash matched it and more," the T-U wrote. "Amid this mania, the idea was promulgated that there was a right-wing extreme just as evil [as communism]."

That assumption was true. Any objective study of McCarthy's un-American actions would justify labeling the senator a right-wing extremist.

McCarthy ruined the lives of thousands of loyal Americans through slander and half-truths, as well as unsubstantiated accusations, later proven false. He accused American heroes such as General George Marshall – architect of the Marshall Plan, which saved many Europeans from the scourge of communism – of being a communist conspirator.

Among those "guilty" of castigating McCarthy were presidents Truman and Eisenhower, Republican Sen. Margaret Chase Smith, Southern conservative Sen. John McClellan, Secretary of the Army Robert Stevens and numerous other Republicans and Democrats. Sen. McClellan denounced "the convicting of people by rumor and hearsay and innuendo."

Also among McCarthy's leading critics was award-winning radio and television journalist Edward R. Murrow. In early 1954, during the Army-McCarthy hearings, Joseph Welch, special counsel to the Army, chastised McCarthy for his vicious attacks, saying: "Senator, have you no sense of decency, sir, at long last?"

By March 1954, McCarthy had become so extreme that

SECTION SIX

Republican Sen. Ralph Flanders accused him of attempting to destroy the GOP and create a one-man party, with McCarthy as its head. Flanders then introduced a resolution in the Senate asking that McCarthy be censured. A select committee was formed with Republican Sen. Arthur Watkins serving as its chairman. On December 2, 1954, based on a 40,000-word report, the Senate voted 67-22 to censure McCarthy for conduct that was "contemptuous, contumacious, denunciatory, unworthy, inexcusable and reprehensible."

Sen. McCarthy first came to my attention in the late 1940s. After serving in the Office of Strategic Services (OSS) during and immediately after World War II, I became editor of a weekly publication printed in Munich for the European Air Transport Service. In that capacity, I covered the Malmedy war crimes trial held at the Dachau Concentration Camp near Munich.

The 74 accused defendants were all members of the 6th SS German Panzer army commanded by Gen. Josef (Sepp) Dietrich. They had been charged with the cold-blooded murder of about 750 American prisoners of war and 150 Belgian civilians. The incidents took place in December 1944 and January 1945 during the last major Nazi counteroffensive, called the Ardennes Offensive, or the Battle of the Bulge.

Of the 74 SS men on trial, including Gen. Dietrich, all but one was found guilty of atrocities. Of these, 43 were sentenced to death. When the trial ended, Sen. McCarthy intervened on the side of the Nazi SS defendants. He accused the U.S. Army of tricking them into confessions. As a result of the

confusion that McCarthy created, not one defendant was executed. Dietrich died at his home in Germany in 1966. What were the facts deliberately overlooked by McCarthy? Gen. Dietrich had issued orders to his SS Panzer Army "That the rules of war would be cast aside, that humane inhibitions would not be shown, that prisoners of war and civilians would be shot." Six American survivors of the massacre who had been left for dead testified at Dachau. They identified some of the SS defendants as participants in the slaughter. When the trial began, the defendants were a carefree, imperturbable group of men. As the evidence against them grew, they became more solemn. I have a set of the prosecution's photos showing the victims in the snow. They had been brutally beaten after being shot.

McCarthy wanted to head a new one-man party. He had already said that all Democrats were either communist followers or sympathizers. His actions proved he wanted to promulgate an extreme right-wing government, dedicated to the destruction of our Constitution, and especially the Bill of Rights.

As Hitler did, McCarthy used the real threats and evils of the communist system to destroy our democracy and establish a dictatorship. Hitler succeeded. Thank goodness McCarthy failed.

The T-U should leave Joseph McCarthy where he belongs – on the trash heap of history.

SECTION SIX

Hitler's Maps

Shortly before I was transferred back to the United States, I was sitting in a restaurant at the Templehof Airport in Germany when I noticed on the tablecloth what appeared to be maps of the English Coastline and a blueprint for a German air-strike by the Luftwaffe. I asked where the tablecloth had come from and the waiter told me that it had been made from old war plans and maps and there were more sheets like it down in the basement. I skipped my meal and went down to the basement to gather as many of these "tablecloths" as I could carry! I later found more in an office in Munich. As it was very close to my time of departure when I made this discovery and I didn't get a chance to publicize it in the Carrier Courier, I brought the maps home with me, planning to share them with the general public someday. "Someday" came more quickly

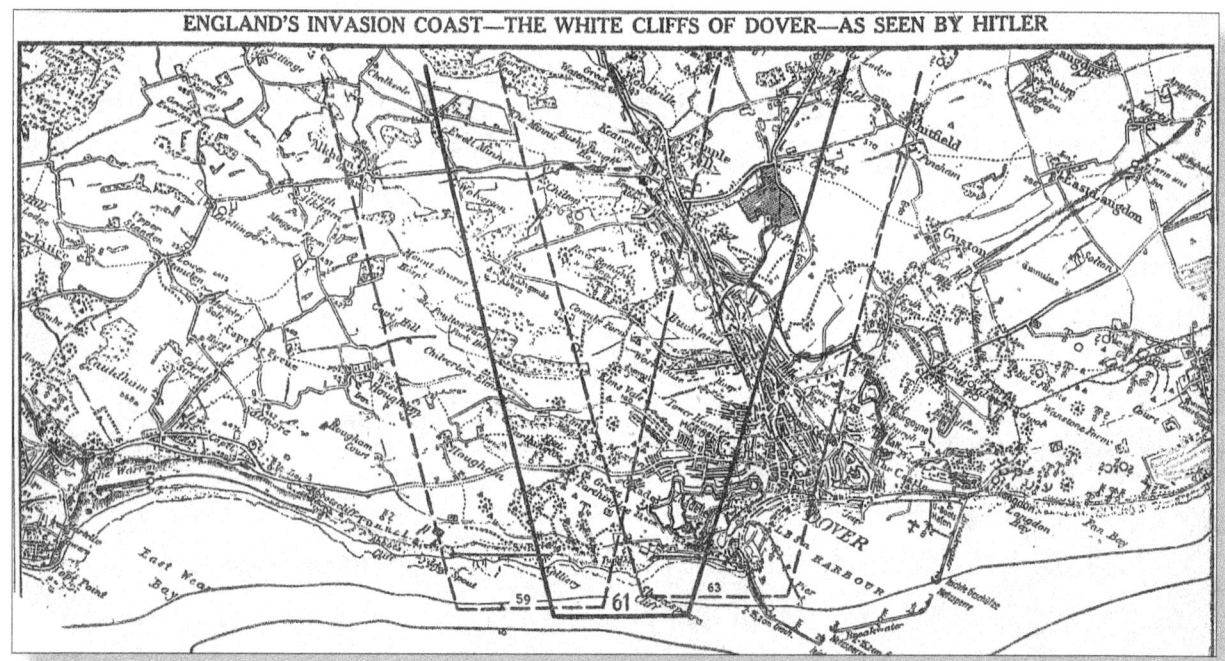

than I had imagined.
On August 18, 1946, the Florida Times-Union in Jacksonville ran an AP article with the headline: **Hitler Blueprint for Invasion of**

England Bared by War Crimes Prosecution Staff. A portion of that article follows:

On August 21, 1946, the Florida Times-Union followed up with an article about my find, detailing the information I had submitted to the newspaper. That article follows:

> Jacksonville Veteran Shows Maps of Nazi Invasion Plan – Thoroughness of Hitler's Preparations for Attack on England Revealed in Charts of Marvin Edwards
>
> The completeness of Adolf Hitler's plans to invade England

SECTION SIX

in 1940 or 1941, and the inadequacies of England's defense against such plans, is strikingly told in a series of air maps prepared by the Luftwaffe just after the fall of France and which were brought to this country recently by Marvin Edwards, a Jacksonville veteran of the Army Air Forces.

The maps and photographs of coastlines and defense installations, all prepared in great detail, fill four thick volumes which apparently had been widely distributed throughout the key units of the German armed forces. From dates included in the reproductions, the aerial photography was accomplished in September 1940, about three months after France surrendered, Germany occupied the Channel ports, and the air battle over England was at its height.

Then all Germany was singing "We're Sailing Against England"; Churchill had told his people: "We will fight on the beaches, on the landing grounds, in the fields and on the hills," and only 700 English Spitfires and Hurricanes stood between an almost helpless nation and the invaders. The history of the war tells now that those "few to whom so many owe so much" did repel the Luftwaffe, climaxing their grim battle by knocking 187 German planes out of the air on September 15, 1940, and ending the German hope of dominating the English skies. But the pictures and plans which had been in the making during that bloody month went to the printers and were distributed two months later while Hitler still had hopes of a successful, if not an easy, invasion. That hope was not completely wrecked until April and May of 1941, when British bombers found and ruined Hitler's invasion fleet of some 3,000 barges and 4,000,000 tons of shipping in Channel ports.

The invasion maps brought to Jacksonville show the southern coast of England from Ramsgate to the Isle of Wight in excellent topographical detail, together with the minutest details of England's invasion defenses including mine fields, barbed wire and concrete coastal barriers, flak installations, gun emplacements, tank traps, fighter airfields and all of the other makeshift devices the English had set up to try to repel what they must have believed to be an irresistible onslaught. The maps show one significant fact – a fact only recently admitted by the English – that only around the English port of Dover, directly across the Channel from France at the Channel's narrowest point, were invasion defenses at all adequate. Such defenses were almost non-existent along the rest of the southern coast, the German surveys showed.

Only last week intelligence officers of the Allied forces released copies of similar maps together with stories of Germany's preparations for invasion and of England's lack of preparedness to repel it.

Edwards, who is the son of Mr. and Mrs. Albert H. Edwards, 1103 River Oaks Road, enlisted in the Army Air Forces in April 1943 and concluded his terminal leave on August 16. He wears the Air Medal with four battle stars, the Presidential Unit Citation, and the various theatre, occupation and victory medals. Following the European armistice, he covered the Malmedy war trials at Dachau, resulting from the German murders of American prisoners taken in the Battle of the Bulge, and also the United Nations meeting in London last January, for his camp newspaper.

SECTION SIX

Marvin's World War II Medals

Now I was back in the U.S.A. with the war behind me and I was expected to begin building my life as a civilian. It was not an easy transition from war-time to peace-time, but there were young men like me all over the country who were doing it. At age 26, I had become hardened by what I had seen and learned in the war. Nothing surprised me anymore and I had some definite insights into the human capacity for savagery. I felt strong enough to handle anything, having become a Humanist. My former faith in God had been shattered by the tragedy of the events I had witnessed. My overwhelming lesson learned from war was that nothing changes. As German Philosopher Georg Wilhelm Friedrich Hegel said, "We learn from history that we do not learn from history." Going forward as an active citizen of the City of Jacksonville, Florida, I became focused on doing all that I could do to make people aware of the atrocities I'd seen in hopes that awareness would somehow lead to prevention of history repeating itself. I eventually adopted Einstein's philosophy: "When I do right, I feel right," and that has served me well for the last seven decades.

Taking on the mantle of being a responsible citizen and using my journalistic experience to bring awareness to the general public of the continuing inequities happening in Germany and elsewhere, I wrote for several local publications. Some articles were published and some were not, but the following is one that I feel compelled to share in this book.

SECTION SIX

MURDER IS THEIR BUSINESS
By Marvin R. Edwards (March 1947)

> With malice toward all if we win,
> With charity for ourselves if we lose,
> With firmness in our military might,
> We strive on to conquer the world,
> For we are the German General Staff.

The German General Staff has triumphed again. After instigating and waging the two most terrible wars in history, this Military Caste was acquitted at Nuremberg on the charges of "crimes against the peace, war crimes, and crimes against humanity."

According to the decision handed down by the International Military Tribunal, only Field Marshall Keital and Colonel General Jodl of the General Staff are specifically charged and guilty. The Tribunal declared that evidence against other members of the General Staff was "clear and convincing," and as an organization it was a "disgrace to the honorable profession of arms" and "ruthless," but nevertheless not guilty.

Only the Russian Judge dissented from the acquittal. Justice Jackson, chief prosecutor for the United States, declared, "Our argument for their conviction, which seemed so convincing to all of us prosecutors, seems not to have made a similar impression on the Tribunal."

The German General Staff was the most powerful group in German political life even before the First World War. In 1914, this Military Caste set into motion the most destructive war machine of its day. Bent on world conquest, the

German Army was ready to march long before the English, French or Russian forces had been mobilized. The German General Staff ordered violations of all accepted standards of international law, and it ordered disregard for the code of "honorable" warfare. It was directly responsible for such wanton acts as the invasion and rape of little Belgium, the sinking of merchant and passenger ships of neutral as well as of belligerent nations, and the introduction of poison gas.

The Treaty of Brest-Litowsk, the harshest treaty of modern times, was imposed by the Military Caste on Russia in March 1918, when it still appeared that Germany might win the war. Under its terms, all of the people of the Baltic States, Russian Poland, and the Ukraine were placed under German "protection." This clause effected fifty-six million people (thirty-two percent of Russia's population), and it took from Russia seventy-three percent of her iron, eighty-nine percent of her coal, and thousands of factories. The Treaty also stipulated that Russia was to subject all of her produce and commerce to the control of the German master. Reparations in gold and goods totaling almost two billion dollars were levied to complete the subjugation of Russia.

Just two years later, the General Staff was crying out against the unjust terms of the Versailles Treaty. They objected to the clause reducing the German Army to 100,000 professional soldiers, limiting arms, and most important, dissolving the General Staff.

Actually, the General Staff did not dissolve. It settled down in the Bendlerstrasse in Berlin, occupying building number fourteen, formerly belonging to the German Admiralty. In October 1919, Major-General Reinhardt became chief of

SECTION SIX

the High Command of the Rechswehr (German Army), and Major General Hans von Seekt chief of the Troops office, which was the camouflaged name of the General Staff.

In January 1921, the still active General Staff was already breaking the disarmament clauses of the Versailles Treaty. The Allies had sent a threat of a more rigid occupation unless the Home Guards and Security Police (both military organizations) were disbanded. These orders were never completely carried out. In Bavaria alone, the Home Guards numbered 320,000, with nearly as many rifles, and about 3,000 machine guns, 44 field guns and 34 mine-throwers.

Added to these "non-professional" military organizations were a number of Free Corps groups and associations such as the Treubund, Olympia, Stahlhelm, Kriegsflagge, and Wehrwolf. Retired or active General Staff officers trained most of these groups. By 1923, when Hitler was meeting failure in his Burgerbrau Putsch, the Military Caste was already rearming Germany for the Second World War. Veterans of the many hundreds of military organizations and short-term trainees in the regular army swelled the list of reserves.

According to the German-Soviet Treaty of 1922 (renewed four years later), arms manufactured in Russia under German supervision were sent to Germany. The General Staff sent large numbers of troops regularly into Russia to train in the use and handling of weapons forbidden Germany. That is, tanks, armored cars, and planes. All this was done during the days of the "democratic" Weimar Republic.

During the period between the wars, the General Staff

ruthlessly suppressed or murdered all those who stood in the way of its objective. Despite this resort to violence, the Military Caste managed to stay out of the public's eye. The "trigger" work was always done by a "tool" who was to take all the blame if something went wrong. The Staff was always able to find a "sucker."

Enough information has been brought to light in recent years to prove conclusively that it was the General Staff and certain industrialists who put the Nazis in power. Had the Military Caste supported one of the other militant organizations, the world would have cursed another German instead of Hitler. The mass of the German people would have backed up any other party that the Staff saw fit to put before them. Such Generals as Fritsch, Brauchitsch, Reichenau, Bock, Rudstedt and the convicted Keitel and Jodl all share equal responsibility for putting the Nazis in power, and leading Germany on the road to war. These officers were working for war, not as individuals, but as members of the General Staff.

The Kaiser and Hitler have disappeared from the international scene. While they have passed from the stage, three constants have remained through both world wars. These are: The German General Staff, the large industrialists, and the German people. As a group all have been smart enough to escape the blame.

The Nuremberg Tribunal has acquitted the General Staff on all counts. The millions of soldiers who died in both world wars dissent, and find them guilty of "crimes against the peace." The martyrs of Lidice, the victims of the concentration camps and the bombings, the murdered prisoners of war,

SECTION SIX

and the enslaved people all cry out the guilt of the German General Staff for "War crimes and crimes against humanity."

Oscar Wilde once wrote, "There is only one thing worse than injustice, and that is justice without a sword in her hand." There may have been a sword at Nuremberg, but its point was certainly dull.

I have always had a special place in my heart for Denmark and a love for the Danish people. King Christian X was a hero who, upon being informed that the Germans were going to invade his country, set about immediately evacuating nearly all of the 20,000 Jews who lived in Denmark. He sent them out in fishing vessels, most of them going to Sweden for the remainder of the war. He managed to rescue about 95% of the Jewish population in Denmark prior to the Nazi's invading. On the 75th Anniversary of the Temple in Copenhagen, King Christian attended the service. I wrote the following essay about his humanity as a monarch and his bravery as a patriot of Denmark.

THE FLAG ON THE TOWN HALL – March 1947
By Marvin R. Edwards

King Christian X of Denmark was a man of great stature. He was the tallest monarch in Europe, being possessed with a height of six feet seven inches. He was also the best loved ruler on the continent.

The Danish ruler always thought of his people, and how he could best serve them. If he had done nothing else, the fact that every morning he could be seen riding majestically around the streets of Copenhagen on his great black horse, with no bodyguards surrounding him, endeared him to his

people. He would stop to talk to a housekeeper cleaning the steps of her home; an elderly man taking a walk; a young girl on her way to school; or a business man. Sometimes he would dismount to play with a group of children. As the King passed the Town Hall each morning, he would salute the Danish flag flying from a staff atop the building.

When Denmark was invaded by the Nazis, King Christian was in his seventieth year. He was warned by the Germans that any resistance would result in the Luftwaffe doing to Copenhagen what it had done to Warsaw. The Germans said that if no violence took place, the Danes could retain their political and administrative institutions unmolested.

The King notified his cabinet of the ultimatum. He expressed his distrust of the Germans, but he added that for the present it would be best to acquiesce. The Cabinet agreed with the King unanimously. King Christian informed the Germans of the decision and he added that he would hold them to their promise that there would be no infringement of the Danish constitution.

The Danish flag continued to fly from the staff atop the Town Hall in Copenhagen. King Christian resumed his daily horseback ride throughout the City. The German troops looked on with amusement at the King who rode among his people with no weapons save a smile and a friendly greeting.

It was a summer's day in 1940. The King was on his way back to the Palace after a refreshing three hour ride around the outskirts of Copenhagen. As he once again passed by the Town Hall, he raised his hand to salute the flag.

SECTION SIX

He stopped short, bringing his arm back down to his side. There would be no salute today. On top of the flagstaff was the red and black German flag.

A German soldier walked by. When he saw the King, he snapped to attention and then threw his arm out in the Nazi salute. King Christian kept his hand at his side. The soldier stood there as the rider rode off at a gallop.
Back at the palace, the King contacted the General who had ordered that the German flag replace the Danish emblem over the Town Hall.

"The German flag is to be taken down," said Christian.

"I ordered it up, and so it shall stay," replied the General.

"Tomorrow morning I will send a Danish soldier to take it down and to replace it with the Danish flag."

"He will never reach the flag pole. I have already placed a sentry by the Town Hall with orders to shoot anyone who attempts to touch the flag."

Christian hung up the phone. He knew that as long as the Danish flag flew from the Town Hall it would give the people hope and courage.

The following morning a soldier on horseback was seen leaving the Palace. He headed straight for the Town Hall. Here he stopped, and dismounted. An armed sentry paraded back and forth in front of the entrance. When he saw the newly arrived soldier, the German snapped to attention. The rider went into the Town Hall and up to the

King Christian

SECTION SIX

roof. Here he met another Nazi sentry who also clicked his heels. The visitor walked over to the flag pole and pulled down the German flag. A few minutes later, a Danish flag was up in its place. The guard started to say something, but he couldn't get the words out. The rider was soon on the street again. He mounted his horse and headed back to the Palace, having taken time out to salute the flag as had been his custom for so many years.

COMMENT ADDED: As the Danish King saluted his flag and mounted his horse, the German guard saluted him silently. No punishment was meted out and the Danish flag continued to fly. Christian X lived to a ripe old age, a respected monarch to the end of his life.

I was still President of White Star Sales Corporation when I met my future wife, Helene Sirota, in Washington, D.C. Helene and I were married in 1955 and by then, realizing that I was not cut out for sales, and upon the advice of my wife and several of my clients (mostly doctors) to whom I provided investment advice, I applied with the S.E.C. for certification as an Investment Counselor. I launched my firm, Edwards & Edwards, Inc. in 1958. By 1961, our three children, Jeffrey, Douglas and Carolyn, had come along. Our life in Jacksonville, Florida has been a lively and fulfilling one, with a great many challenges, sorrows, struggles and joys along the way.

Today, Helene and I enjoy our good health and our fine family, which now includes seven grandchildren, and we look back on the years with amazement. How the years have flown by ... almost as swiftly and undetected as the OSS Mosquito I once navigated over enemy territory. There is an old Chinese Curse: "May You Live in Interesting Times." Have we been cursed? Judge for yourself.

SECTION SEVEN

OSS REUNION

WW II 50th Anniversaries Begin

The Summer and Fall of 1993 saw the start of numerous 50th Anniversary Celebrations of various military components of OSS and allied operatives that participated in clandestine actions of WWII. The first such was that of the "CARPETBAGGERS" – the US Airmen who flew our missions and resistance supplies from England into Europe – whose exceptional Reunion took place in England and France. The following is an "abbreviated account of 10 of the most fully packed memorable days imaginable," as reported by LTC J. W. "Brad" Bradbury, a San Antonio based Air Force historian who organized and realized this unique Anniversary.

"CAN YOU SCRAMBLE?"

That question during WW II over the scramble phone to the "Carpetbaggers" operations officer indicated the beginning of another special air mission to the Resistance. In 1993, it signaled the start of a reunion/anniversary – a never before and never again meeting between French Maquisards and American/British special air operations folk.

August 27th marked the beginning when eighty or so assembled in England at the Kettering Park Hotel, Northampton. On the 28th the little known but well remembered Gibralter Farm (Tempsford), where the old "Joe" barn is still standing, witnessed the planting of a memorial tree among the others. The plaque for this one identified the first "Carpetbagger" lost on a mission flying from Tempsford in November 1943.

SECTION SEVEN

Marvin & Helene – Kettering Park Hotel, Northampton, England

On the 29th at Harrington, site of the main "Carpetbagger" air base, U.S. and RAF wreaths were placed at the monument (a P-52 flew by in salute) and the new "Carpetbagger" Museum was dedicated. It is housed in the old operations building and is more remarkable since it was done by the farmer who now owns the place and a few of his friends – and it is excellent. Our English visit was highlighted that night by a banquet at the Kettering Park Hotel.

Then, on the 30th, we flew to Paris, the introduction to France (on the ground) for most of the "Carpetbaggers." They were welcomed as VIPs by the Mayor at the Hotel de Ville and by the Order of the Liberation at the Hotel des invalids and Arc de Triomphe. At the Arc, the French Air Force band played, the Gendarmes blocked off the Champs-Elysees, and "Carpetbaggers," carrying a wreath and American Flag, led the column of Resistance associations to the Tomb of the Unknown Soldier.

Marvin signing register at Arc de Triomphe Ceremony in Paris – 1993

Then on to Lyon, the headquarters for the reception, commemoration and meals in the hills to the west and east for the next five days. Here in the Loire, many people, French, Belgian, British and American, joined with the "Carpetbaggers." The ceremonies, wine, food and warmth of welcome defy description. At St. Cyr de Valorges, 18 French and American cadets from L'Ecole de L'Air Salon participated in the ceremonies and were welcomed. The Commander-in-Chief, U.S. Air Forces Europe, came to Duerne to meet Maquisards and "Carpetbaggers" and to honor the crew and the Resistance members memorialized by the monument there.

At Izenore, where the first "Carpetbagger" C-47 landed in Occupied France, the French had a surprise in store. There was considerable questioning as to why so many people (at least 250) were gathered there for what was billed as a picnic. The answer came when a large marble monument was unveiled, commemorating the

SECTION SEVEN

1943 event. The dedication of this fifth monument in France to the "Carpetbaggers" was a fitting climax to the ten-day reunion/anniversary, packed with affection, honor and appreciation from the hundreds of French people, young and old. Yes, we could scramble.

Nous Nous Souvenons de Nos Camarades!

OSS Reunion 1993 – Members of OSS

OSS Reunion Stories

We spent a week going to many small towns in the Lyon area. Ceremonies were held at all the sites where our aircraft had crashed, while dropping supplies to the resistance forces. The French had built memorials with the names of the crew members carved into the monuments. Both French and American generals participated in the ceremonies. Needless to say, they were emotional affairs, bringing back memories of the struggle that took place almost 50 years earlier.

Marvin & Helene at OSS Memorial in Cyr de Valorges, France – 9-2-93

SECTION SEVEN

There was a small town in France, St. Cyr de Valorges, where the town square was named after an American Soldier, James H. Heddleson. Heddleson was shot down and hid in a barn until he was found by a village woman who took him in. Dressed in peasant clothes, the young soldier stayed in the village and worked in the French underground during the war. He stayed until he was rescued by the Allies. The people were so excited to see Americans when we arrived that they backed up a panel truck and handed out loaves of French Bread, yelling "Jimmy, Jimmy, Jimmy!" We were wined and dined royally.

The most wonderful aspect of our 50th reunion of the OSS was the careful planning done by our hosts, the Bradbury's, having gone the year before and mapped out all of the places where our OSS heroes had fallen. We were able to visit each of those places and pay a proper tribute to them.

SECTION EIGHT
AWARDS AND RECOGNITIONS

04-25-13 Marvin Edwards received medal for French Knight of Legion of Honor from the French Ambassador to the United States Francois Delattre.

Family at Marvin's Awards Ceremony

SECTION EIGHT

Three Letters of Support for Legion of Honor

12 June 2012

Consulat general de France a Miami
Espirito Santo Plaza, Suite 1050
1395 Brickell Avenue
Miami, FL. 33131

Re: Legion of Honor for Marvin Edwards

To Whom It May Concern,

To the men and women of CIA, the men and women of OSS are both heroes and pioneers. Heroes for the part they played in the defeat of evil in Europe and Asia. Pioneers for the example and experience they provided to American espionage in the Cold War and beyond. The space afforded by this short letter cannot capture the full contributions of OSS, let alone the individual acts of strength and valor that are such a rich and moving part of its legacy. OSS was a remarkable organization of clarity and conviction, of resolve and results.

In Europe and Asia, OSS units reached out to resistance movements, providing them equipment, leadership, and the vital reassurance that in their fight against oppression, they were neither forgotten nor alone. Mr. Marvin Edwards, in his capacity as a navigator with the 492nd Bomb Group, flew in support of OSS air operations to drop allied agents and supplies into France during WWII. He has been an active contributor to our historical programs for more than a decade. We have especially valued consulting with him regarding his experience with CIA's predecessor, the Office of Strategic Services. His personal anecdotes and sharing of lessons learned during Carpetbagger missions to drop agents and supplies into France enriched our understanding of OSS operations with the French Resistance as only a personal recounting of such experiences could. His loan of his own photo archives and documents has enhanced our ability to recount through our exhibits the authentic stories that continue to inspire our officers and provide them a better understanding of WWII air operations. His willingness to share his extensive knowledge and historical contributions continues to inform, instruct and inspire current and future generations of intelligence officers and for this we are most grateful.

On behalf of <u>all</u> who continue the vital missions begun decades ago by that remarkable generation of remarkable Americans, I fully support his consideration for the Legion of Honor in recognition of his wartime service in France.

Sincere regards,

Toni Hiley

Toni L. Hiley
CIA Museum Director

...ideas
defining
a free
society

June 8, 2012

Consulate General of France
Espirito Santo Plaza, Suite 1050
1395 Brickell Avenue
Miami, FL
33131

To Whom It May Concern,

I write in support of Mr. Marvin Edwards' application for the Legion of Honor. In 2008, Mr. Edwards generously donated his collection of historical materials documenting the activities of the 492nd Bomb Group during World War II to the Hoover Institution Library and Archives. This collection details not only his service as a Navigator with the United States Army Air Forces, but also his work with the Office of Strategic Services (OSS) in support of resistance forces within occupied Europe. Working in this capacity for the Office of Strategic Services (OSS), Mr. Edwards had a special relationship with various members of the French underground. Due to his generous gift, this material is open and available to future researchers interested in the topic.

Thank you for your consideration. If I can be of further assistance, please do not hesitate to contact me directly.

Sincerely,

Danielle Scott
Library and Archives Collections Manager
Hoover Institution
Stanford University
Stanford, CA 94305-6010

SECTION EIGHT

Consulat General de France
Espirito Santo Plaza
Suite 1050
1395 Brickell Avenue
Miami, FL 33131

June 18, 2012

Dear Consul General,

It is with great admiration and support that I recommend Marvin Edwards to you.

Mr. Edwards is highly regarded in the City of Jacksonville and by all who know him. He is a fearless and tireless advocate for truth and integrity. Mr. Edwards has devoted his career to holding elected and appointed public leaders to the highest standards of honesty. He expects no less from those in private positions of power and influence.

Mr. Edwards devotes his time, resources and formidable communications skills to those who need him in the pursuit of justice and fair treatment.

Mr. Edwards is legendary for his ability and willingness to speak out against injustice, regardless of the political fallout that might occur. In fact, he strives to engage those in power so that they respond to his insightful and well-researched questions and concerns. He demands no less than full accountability.

As a personal friend, Marvin, his wife, Helene, and his three wonderful children are unequaled. They are kind, generous, understanding and loyal.

It is a pleasure to provide my full support for Marvin Edwards.

Sincerely,

Karen Brune Mathis

Karen Brune Mathis
Managing Editor
The Financial News & Daily Record

SPECIAL FORCES ASSOCIATION

This is to certify that

MARVIN R. EDWARDS

Has been accepted as a member of the
Special Forces Association

This **17th** Day of **February 2017**

Cliff Newman
Administrative Director

Carolyn Edwards
February 6

Allowed on Timeline

My father, Marvin R. Edwards, was honored this weekend by members of a local chapter of Special Ops veterans from OSS, the CIA, the Green Berets and Navy Seals...very proud! — with Marvin R. Edwards and Helene Edwards.

Tag Photo   Suggest Location

Like   Comment   Share

Adam Edwards, Doug Edwards and 21 others

Carolyn Edwards Chris Oliveri Michael Oliveri Mary Boehmer Edwards Doug Edwards Kristen Edwards Adam Edwards Avalon Edwards Nathaniel Edwards Terese Karmel Ina Tornberg Joan Gurevich Bill Wainger Gerry Gurevich Martin Jay

Write a comment...

SECTION EIGHT

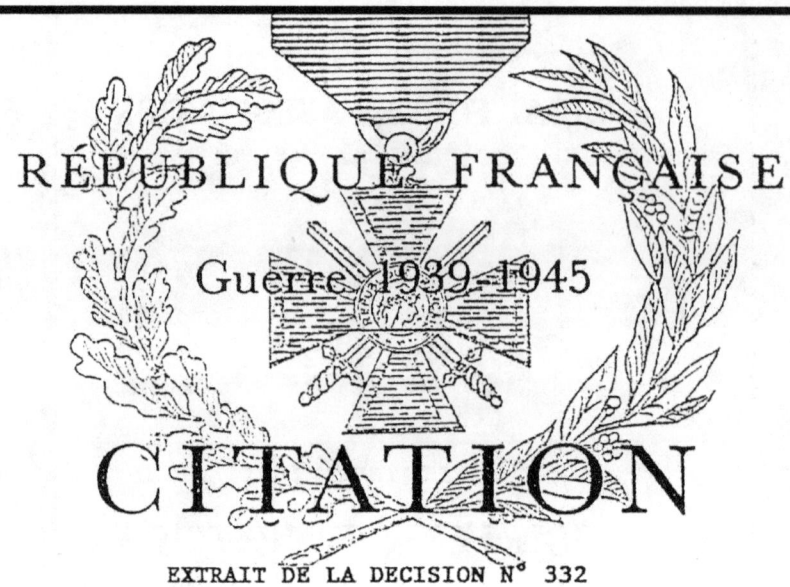

RÉPUBLIQUE FRANÇAISE
Guerre 1939-1945

CITATION

EXTRAIT DE LA DECISION N° 332

LE PRESIDENT DU GOUVERNEMENT PROVISOIRE DE LA REPUBLIQUE FRANCAISE,

CITE A L'ORDRE DE L'ARMEE

the 492nd Bombardment Group (H)

A magnificent unit, distinguishing itself by its determination, its bravery and its spirit of sacrifice.

During the period from January 4 to September 17, 1944, effected, on unprotected aircraft, more than 2,000 day and night missions over enemy occupied French territory. These flights assured, under conditions rendered perilous by aerial combat and very vigilant enemy ground forces, numerous deliveries by parachute of arms and supplies which greatly aided the Free French forces.

Contributed greatly thus to the allied war effort and to the liberation of France.

THESE CITATIONS ACCOMPANY THE AWARDING OF THE CROIX DE GUERRE (War Cross Medal) 1939-1945 WITH PALM.

Paris, le 17 septembre 1946

Pour ampliation
Le Général d'Armé JUIN
Chef d'Etat-Major Général
de la Défense Nationale
Signé : A. JUIN

Signé : BIDAULT

EXTRAIT CERTIFIE CONFORME
Paris, le 26 AOUT 1987
Pour le Ministre et par autorisation
le Chef du Bureau des Décorations

J.P. GROSSO

THE SPECIAL FORCES CLUB

KNIGHTSBRIDGE
LONDON SW1

MONDAY · DECEMBER 26, 2016 The Times-Union A-6

jacksonville.com/opinion

opinion

Cheers: Marvin Edwards

Honored by Congress

It's pretty cool to get an award when you're 95. But then Marvin Edwards has been doing the unusual for many years.

Edwards was part of a community group that put a spotlight on Jacksonville's failing public schools that led to disaccreditation in the 1960s.

For many years, the financial consultant used his expertise to fight for good government in this city.

He was courageous when he was a lone voice.

In World War II his bravery involved being a lieutenant in the Army Air Force. He was a navigator on a mission deep into Nazi Germany one night in 1945 for the Office of Strategic Services, the precursor of the CIA.

The plane, built mostly of plywood, flew high above German anti-aircraft fire at a speed of more than 400 miles an hour, wrote Times-Union reporter Sandy Strickland in 2013.

For his contributions to the liberation of France, Edwards was awarded the French Legion of Honor medal.

Now Edwards will be one of the OSS alumni honored by an act of Congress.

A bill was passed to award the Congressional Gold Medal to the surviving OSS members.

There are fewer than 100 surviving members of this brave unit, said Sen. Mark Warner, D-Va., in The Washington Times.

While many of the stories of the OSS are not widely known, one of them was made into a movie, "Inglorious Bastards."

According to the bill passed by Congress, Gen. Dwight Eisenhower credited the OSS covert operations in France to the equivalent of having an extra military division.

Another little known fact is that women made up one-third of the OSS personnel.

One OSS operation rescued 500 downed airmen trapped behind enemy lines in Yugoslavia.

Other missions saved the lives of thousands of prisoners of war before they were murdered by the Japanese.

Next year marks the 75th anniversary of the founding of the OSS.

Thankfully, Jacksonville has its own living OSS member. Congratulations to Edwards.

Though this award has come long after most of the OSS members have died, as we like to say, it's never too late to do the right thing.

SECTION NINE

REFLECTIONS

Modern Writings of Marvin Edwards
(21st Century Homer Lea)

Turning Points
Marvin R. Edwards (April 2017)

Before World War II, I was a strong supporter of General Billy Mitchell. He demonstrated that bomber aircraft could sink a battleship. Mitchel was also strongly supported by Major Alexander P. Seversky, a good friend. In 1942, Seversky published a best-selling book called <u>Victory Through Air Power</u>.

Seversky noted, with few exceptions, battleships and even aircraft carriers were sunk by aircraft bombings or by torpedoes fired from the air or from submarines. Seversky noted that the British battleships, "Repulse" and "Prince of Wales" were sunk by a surprise attack by Japanese bombers and fighters. That was like the attack on Pearl Harbor.

Japan appeared to be winning the war in the Pacific. That changed on June 4, 1942. A major Japanese fleet, including aircraft carriers, was headed toward Midway Island, expecting to occupy that strategic island. They were surprised by our fleet, including the only three aircraft carriers we had left in the Pacific after Pearl Harbor. They were the "Hornet," "Yorktown," and the "Enterprise." Hidden by clouds, 37 dauntless dive bombers from the Enterprise attacked the Japanese fleet. Three of Japan's top aircraft carriers were sunk. A fourth was badly damaged and then sank. What was left of the Japanese fleet limped back to Japan. After Midway, Japan was put on the defensive. That was the turning point in the Pacific.

SECTION NINE

Just as the Battle of Midway from June 3rd through 6th, 1942, put Japan from a successful aggressor nation to a nation concerned about holding all the land they had seized and protecting their home islands from attack, Germany's downfall began after its peak was reached when France surrendered to the Germans, causing Hitler and his generals to think that England would be a pushover.

The Germans occupied the French channel ports that brought them closer to the coast of England, and the only real defense England had was about 700 fighter aircraft, mostly Spitfires and Hurricanes. Prime Minister Churchill stated, "We will fight on the beaches, on the surrounding grounds, in the fields and in the hills." Only Britain's fighter aircraft stood in the way of the expected invasion.

A major air battle took place between August 8 and October 31, 1940. In what has been called the Battle of Britain, a massive attack by hundreds of Luftwaffe fighters and bombers was met by the Royal Air Force. At the end, about 562 German aircraft were shot down, compared to 139 RAF airplanes. That was a major blow to the Luftwaffe and the planned invasion of England.

Hitler felt that the destruction of his airpower would only delay the invasion. In April 1941, British bombers attacked about 3,000 troop barges in the channel. That put an end to the planned invasion of England. As noted it was to have taken place on the coast of England between the Islands of Wight and Dover. From that point on, Germany was on the defensive.

One last attempt by the Germans took place in the period between December 1944 and January 1945. The surprise attack became known as the "Battle of the Bulge." The attack was halted when Allied bombers destroyed the fuel storage area for the tanks' fuel supply. Unable to move, the tanks were targets for bombings.

Without the more than 1,000 tanks, the Allies counter-attacked and the Germans involved gave up.

Thus, the Battle of the Midway with the sinking of Japanese aircraft carriers, and the Battle of Britain, illustrating the inability of German troops to invade England, I consider the turning points in World War II.

The Papertrail
by Marvin Edwards – 11.05.02
Painful Lessons
As history shows,
appeasing rogue nations can be fatal

Numerous Washington D.C. officials expressed surprise that North Korea confirmed what the CIA had earlier reported: that they were secretly developing nuclear weapons. The action violated North Korea's accord with the United States, reached in 1994 and 1995, in which they agreed to demolish their military nuclear facilities. The U.S., in turn, offered to give the country two nuclear reactors for power generation. The reactors were designed to use a grade of plutonium difficult to convert into weapons use.

Supporters of the deal were naïve to trust the leaders of a ruthless totalitarian state. Breaking international agreements is nothing new. Failure of the League of Nations to take punitive action against violators following World War I encouraged aggression by Germany, Japan and Italy, and led to World War II. The resulting cost was measured by the slaughter of millions of soldiers and civilians along with trillions of dollars' worth of destruction.*

*Still relevant today!

SECTION NINE

WWII led to the demise of the League as a credible international body, but the United Nations has also been gutless. Since the UN was established, there have been numerous wars, declared and undeclared, resulting in the death of millions of civilians. They have taken place in Asia, Africa, the Middle East and South America. The UN has been impotent, refusing to punish major treaty transgressions.

Here follows a list of some of the most significant violations since World War I, and the current crisis: In 1919, after WWI, a defeated Germany signed the Treaty of Versailles, but most terms were never enforced. Only an insignificant sum of the original $32 billion reparations payment was ever made and the elimination of the German General Staff didn't happen. Instead, their membership increased. The Rhineland industrial area between France and Germany was to remain demilitarized. In March 1936, Hitler ordered his army to occupy the zone, annexing it to Germany. Neither France nor the League demanded that Germany withdraw from the area.

In 1922, Japan was a signatory to the Washington Naval Disarmament Agreement, requiring it to limit the size and quantity of naval ships. Japan ignored the agreement, accelerating construction of battleships and carriers. This blatant violation was reported, but there were few official protests, also ignored by Japan.

After Hitler occupied Austria in March 1938, he turned his attention to the Sudetenland, part of neighboring democratic Czechoslovakia. Hitler claimed there were 3.5 million Germans there who were being mistreated and demanded the land be ceded to Germany. The Sudeten

contained all the Czech fortifications facing Germany. It also contained the Skoda Armament Works, one of the largest such operations in Europe. Both France and Russia had a pact with the Czechs under which they would go to war against Germany if the Germans attacked Czechoslovakia. Britain said they would join France in such a war.

On Aug. 28, 1938, an emergency high-level meeting took place in Munich. In attendance were Hitler, the Italian dictator Benito Mussolini, British Prime Minister Neville Chamberlain, and French Prime Minister Eduard Daladier. Both Chamberlain and Daladier capitulated to Hitler. The infamous Munich Agreement was signed by all four leaders, giving Germany the entire Sudetenland. The Czechs were neither invited to the meeting nor consulted. Chamberlain proclaimed "Peace in our time." Hitler agreed that Germany had no more territorial demands, including the balance of Czechoslovakia. Exactly six months later, in March 1939, Germany occupied the rest of the Czech Republic. In Sept. 1939, Germany invaded Poland, starting WWII. Appeasing militaristic regimes only whets their appetites for aggression.

Those responsible for the tragedy of 9/11 and other brutal actions since then cannot be reasoned with. They are dedicated to the destruction of democracy and Western civilization. Most of Western Europe and the United Nations have not learned from the Munich fiasco. Appeasement continues to this day. We missed the boat by not eliminating Saddam Hussein in the 1991 Gulf War. Eternal vigilance, not just in words, but in deeds, is key to our survival.

SECTION NINE

Today, at age 95, I continue to be a student of history and world affairs. It is in my nature to seek answers to questions that have plagued humanity since the beginning of time, but my research generally leads me to the reasons why certain conflicts have occurred during my lifetime ... wars, genocides, tragedies, inequities in government, misspent funds ... the list is endless. My focus has always been on how these conflicts could have been avoided and how we might learn from our mistakes and do better in the future. Of course, there have been some shining moments in my long life, too ... family and friends ... some battles fought and won on the local scene ... the beauty and power of the written word ... and, of course, the OSS. As a young Air Force Officer and a competent navigator, I was chosen to participate in OSS missions during the last months of World War II. I volunteered to continue as an OSS operative following the war because I knew that what we were doing was important in post-war Europe. Keeping accurate records has always been part of my persona. I believe it is imperative to record history accurately in the hope that it will be acknowledged and the negative aspects of it will not be repeated. Even as a boy, I loved spending time in museums and during the past few decades, I have shared copies of my carefully compiled memorabilia of World War II with the CIA Museum in Washington, D.C., The National World War II Museum in New Orleans, and the Hoover Institute at Stanford University in California. Each of these museums has expressed their appreciation for my contributions (as evidenced by the letters below) and I'm gratified that I was able to provide materials that might not have been available otherwise.

MUSEUM

24 June 2011

Dear Mr. Edwards,

On the occasion of your 90th birthday celebration, your friends at CIA Museum send you warmest greetings and best wishes. We hope the celebration of this notable date finds you well and surround by all those your hold dear.

Your support to CIA Museum over the years has been critical to our understanding of OSS operations during World War II. Thank you for so generously sharing your knowledge of the Joan Eleanor communications system and for the written contribution to its history we include in our OSS collection. Your WWII service honors our republic and your dedication to preserving the history of our WWII predecessor honors the CIA.

Thank you for helping CIA Museum to insure that the daring do of the men and women of the OSS remains accessible to current and future generations of intelligence officers.

Wishing you much happiness and health as you celebrate this very special day! You will always be able to include CIA Museum staff among your greatest admirers!

Very best regards,

Toni L. Hiley
CIA Museum Director
RM 4F50 OHB
Washington, DC 20505

SECTION NINE

*...ideas
defining
a free
society*

June 15, 2011

Dear Mr. Edwards,

Thank you very much for the box of publications and documents that you sent to my attention on June 2, which you collected during your service in the O.S.S. in World War II.

Although some of these publications were already available in the Hoover Institution Library (such as *5 Years: The Occupation of Denmark in Pictures* or *Order of Battle of the German Army*), nevertheless many of them were not, and we will be pleased to add them to our collections. It is likely that many of the documents, articles, and maps will be added to the existing archival collection that is under your name, whereas some of the publications will be cataloged separately in the Hoover Institution Library. In either case, we are pleased that you shared these materials with us and are glad that they will be able to be used by students and scholars.

I would also like to extend congratulations and best wishes on your 90th birthday. Perhaps you will not see this letter until you return from your celebration in Maryland, but I hope that you will have had a very enjoyable time with your family, and that it will be a happy occasion that you and your family will long remember.

In the meantime, if you have any other questions that I or my colleagues can be of assistance with, please feel free to let us know. Thank you once again for your continued interest in and support of the Hoover Institution Library and Archives.

With best wishes,

Sincerely,

Brad Bauer
Associate Archivist for Collection Development

HOOVER INSTITUTION ♦ STANFORD UNIVERSITY ♦ STANFORD, CALIFORNIA 94305-6010 ♦ WWW.HOOVER.ORG

THE NATIONAL
WWII MUSEUM

12 December 2011

Dear Mr. Edwards,

I just wanted to thank you again for your time and for sharing your wartime experiences with me. Tom Gibbs, the other Historian who met with us in the library before your interview, is still talking about the articles you wrote before the war. He was very impressed with them as was I. I was also very impressed with the maps you have and sincerely hope you are still considering passing on a set of them to us.

The DVD copy of the interview we conducted here at the museum back in October just contains the raw footage from the interview. What we shot is what's on the disk. The interview has not been edited in any way. Also, the DVD is not coded so you should have no trouble making copies if you desire to do so. If by some chance you do encounter problems trying to copy the DVD just give me a call or email and will be more than happy to make additional copies for you.

Thank you again for your time Mr. Marvin and thank you very much for your service. Please do not hesitate to call, write, or email if you have any questions, comments, or additional information to share.

Happy Holidays to you and your family.

Sincerely,

Joey Balfour
Historian/Curator
The National WWII Museum
945 Magazine Street
New Orleans, LA 70130-3813
Phone: 504-528-1944 ext. 286
Toll Free: 877-813-3329 ext. 286
Email: joey.balfour@nationalww2museum.org

The War That Changed The World
The National World War II Museum | 945 Magazine Street | New Orleans, LA 70130-3813 | Phone 504.528.1944 | Fax 504.586.8553 | www.nationalww2museum.org

SECTION NINE

As Historian and Curator of The National WWII Museum, Mr. Balfour's comments about my articles written before the war were particularly gratifying to me. I've long admired prophets like Homer Lea and have, a few times, been correct in my assessment of the outcome of a future event. This I do not consider a gift, but simply the result of extensive research and a great deal of focused reasoning. My research and reasoning continues to this day. I am still as interested in our history and our future as I've ever been. In writing this book, I've reminisced about so many of the occurrences that might not have happened had the leaders of our country listened to the thinkers.

For instance, I've been researching again about the numerous warnings that were made regarding the imminent attack of Pearl Harbor and the Philippines by the Japanese. These warnings were made over a period of 32 years and received little or no publicity. I've discussed some of those warnings in the body of this book.

Another concern that I've pointed out in this book was our invasion of Vietnam. It was a double-cross of the Vietnamese who helped us fight the Japanese in World War II. The cost in American lives came to almost 60,000 in our military and hundreds of thousands of Vietnamese men, women and children were slaughtered. Their help in World War II was kept quiet. Besides the loss of lives, the cost ran into billions of dollars. Now those details have been told in this book.

There are few of us "OSS Carpetbaggers" left today, but my friend, Bill Becker in San Diego, California, has kept the "Carpetbagger" Newsletter (801st/492nd Bombardment Group Association) going and has also been in charge of our annual reunions for many years. Most recently, in the latest "Carpetbagger" Newsletter, Bill published a long article featuring yours truly!

-801st / 492nd BOMBARDMENT GROUP-

CARPETBAGGER

SPRING AND SUMMER EDITION 2017 **NEWSLETTER VOLUME #153**

 *By the full moon we flew*
Secret Wings of the OSS in WW 2

SECTION NINE

Carpetbaggers Operating from HARRINGTON

Joan and Eleanor

The only link with Harrington was the Joe's radio mentioned earlier. The Joan - Eleanor system was specifically developed for Red Stocking Operations by two US radio technicians, Lt. Comdr. Stephen Simpson and Dewitt R. Goddard of the Radio Corporation of America - the code name referring to one's wife and the other's girlfriend.

The system operated on 260 MHz, a frequency free at that time of enemy surveillance stations. The small "Joan" agent's set had a range of about 20 miles. He was given a specific time, usually in the evening to transmit his report, which he did in plain language, the message being received by a radioman hunched in a small cabin installed in the rear fuselage of a De Havilland Mosquito orbiting above at 30,000 ft.

The "Eleanor" equipment on the mosquito was fitted with a wire recorder and the designers claimed that the voice recording could receive in 20 minutes what would take three days by coded Morse. Garbles and mistakes could be clarified on the spot. The original intention was to use B-17 Fortresses for the "Eleanor" but stooging around Germany unescorted, they were assured by the air force was not to be recommended in a Fortress.

The Mosquito was thought ideal for the purpose, so a small batch of PRXVIs were acquired from Hatfield and fitted out at the USAAF base at Watton where the American 654th Reconnaissance unit used the type for tactical intelligence missions. Red Stocking agent missions had a high priority and the 492nd Group at Harrington was chosen to carry out both the A-26 and Mosquito operations. The radio operator access was through a small door cut into the starboard side of the mosquito rear fuselage. He was provided with a heated suit and had an interphone link with the pilot. Long range wing mounted fuel tanks gave sufficient range for most missions. On very long runs they could overfly to an OSS field in Italy.

Popular Missions

The first Mosquitoes to arrive at Harrington were written off by enthusiastic pilots unfamiliar with the pronounced swing on take-off, but former commanding officer Bob Fish remembered that once the pilots mastered the new ships, everyone wanted to fly the Red Stocking trips.

MARVIN EDWARDS, A USAAF MOSQUITO NAVIGATOR ON RED STOCKING MISSIONS WITH THE 492ND BG COMMENTS:

I have noted the description of the Red Stocking missions. It mentions the A-26 aircraft as the plane used. Please be advised that it was found that the British Mosquito aircraft was superior to the A-26 for these missions. That plane could fly faster and at a higher altitude than the A-26. The Mosquito flew at an altitude up to 40,000 feet at a speed of up to 450 miles per hour. It's crew consisted of a pilot and a navigator (I was a navigator on the Red Stocking missions almost to the end of the war in April 1945.) Only one OSS operator in the belly of the plane was required, In fact, several years ago, I wrote an article on Red Stocking missions for the Mosquito Air Crew Association publication. I never flew in an A-26 on these missions.

A year ago, the History Channel on cable TV did a 45-minute special on the Mosquito. It mentioned its use for the Red Stocking Joan/Eleanor missions. The article I wrote for the Mosquito Air Crew Association was reprinted in the Carpetbagger News Letter earlier this year. I might mention the Mosquito had two Rolls Royce Merlin engines for the Red Stocking missions. The plane was made out of plywood. I would greatly appreciate your adding this information to your web site.

Thanks. Marvin R. Edwards   More on Marvin Edwards Go to Pages 4 and 5

Mosquito Aircraft early 1945 Harrington Army Air Field Base in England used in Carpetbagger "Red Stocking" missions over Germany for OSS using Joan / Eleanor equipment (Communications) 492nd Bomb Group.
Marvin R Edwards was navigator.

Helene and Marvin **Marvin relaxing at home**

SECTION NINE

Dec. 7, 1941 was a day Marvin Edwards, 95, and America will never forget.

The bombing of Pearl Harbor -- and the rise of Adolf Hitler in Europe -- prompted Edwards to join the Air Force.
"Germany had seized almost all of Europe and treated the people brutally," he said.
Edwards was part of a special American group called Office of Strategic Services or OSS. It's now known as the CIA.
During that time, Edwards rode in a legendary two-engine British aircraft called the De Havilland Mosquito. The aircraft, known for its blistering speed, was made almost entirely out of wood and was used for spy and reconnaissance missions.

Marvin Cadet

Marvin Navigator

The "Mossie" and crew; Front:(L-R Navigators. Lt. Kolzacki and Lt. Marvin Edwards, Rear: Pilots Lt. Webb, Lt. Ralph Smith and Lt. Kuntz

They worked with American spies in Germany, and are said to have provided crucial information that led to victory.
"The action of OSS and all its pervasive activities on the ground and in the air helped to bring the war to a quicker close," Edwards said.
Edwards' bravery will soon be honored when the OSS receives the Congressional Gold Medal in 2017.
The United States was behind in honoring the OSS and let the French beat them to it. The Society of the French Legion of Honor gave him the award in 2013. "It was something I felt should have been earlier, not just for me, but for thousands of other OSS personnel,
Even though the war was more than 70 years ago, Edwards remembers every detail. He's sharp, a former writer, and retired as little as 10 years ago as an investment counselor. Nowadays, he's taking it easy and counting his blessings. To this hero, age is nothing but a number.
"For 95, I'm doing damn good," he said with a smile.
Edwards said there are fewer than 100 servicemen and women in the OSS who are still alive.

04-25-13 Marvin Edwards received the French Knight of Legion of Honor medal from Ambassador to the United States François Delattre.

5

Congress has passed a bill to award a Congressional Gold Medal to surviving OSS operatives in a ceremony on Capitol Hill in 2017. I'm one of that group and hope the OSS Society will succeed in its plan to build the National Museum of Intelligence and Special Operations to educate the American public about OSS and its successor organizations.I look forward to receiving that Congressional Gold Medal this year that marks our 75th Anniversary. The OSS Spearhead (symbolizing the fact that we were at the tip of the spear defending America) pointed the way forward in war and it has helped to point the way forward for me in life.

Wild Bill Donovan
The Spymaster Who Created the OSS
and Modern American Espionage

from the book by
Douglas Waller

(National Archives)

ADDENDUM I

Homer Lea
The Valor of Ignorance – *The Day of the Saxon*

General Homer Lea

My study of Homer Lea's writings began in 1944, soon after I enlisted in the Air Force. As a student of history with a strong fascination and predilection for predicting future events based on present conditions, I found Homer Lea's books to be well-researched and prophetic.

The following information about Homer Lea was gathered from a book by Richard O'Connor titled Pacific Destiny, An Informal History of the U.S. in the Far East.

Born November 7, 1876, Homer Lea was an American adventurer, author and geo-political strategist. Lea, who was visually impaired,

ADDENDUM I

a hunchback, and no more than five feet tall, spent his boyhood pretending to be a soldier despite the realization that he would never be able to join the military. By the time he reached high school, he had become a military scholar, able to reel off details of historic military battles and even staging replicas of great battles and campaigns in his California backyard. Fiercely independent, Lea refused to be viewed as a "cripple," instead acting as a leader of men in backyard battles and accompanying friends on hiking trips in the mountains.

As a teenager, Homer Lea became fascinated with China, studying its language and history and spending a great deal of time in the Los Angeles Chinatown. Possibly one of the reasons for his interest in China was the fact that the Chinese had a reverence for hunchbacks, believing them to be especially endowed by heaven with wisdom and good luck. Traditionally, Chinese scholars were pictured as "bent-backed" from their studies, thus the Chinese proverb that a man's brains are in his back.

Lea was at Stanford University when the Spanish-American War broke out and was heartbroken to be turned down by the military, even during a war emergency. He joined a college cavalry troop of other misfits, and became known for dressing in flamboyant costumes that accented oriental and military garb, and calling himself the "Martial Monk." Defiant and proud, he became one of the best fencers on campus, and was an expert at poker and chess, always drawing analogies between chess and war. During his last year at Stanford, Lea became close friends with two Chinese-American students, Allen Chung and Lou Hoy, whose wealthy parents lived in China. After many forays with Lea into San Francisco's Chinatown, Chung and Hoy confided in him that they were revolutionaries, and inducted Lea into their secret society whose purpose it was to overthrow the Manchus. Finally, his desire to become a respected

warrior was satisfied! The Chinese valued brains over brawn and hoped that Lea would help garner the American support they needed for their cause. Lea left Stanford to become a soldier of fortune on behalf of a republican China. He applied to the State Department to send him to China as an official observer, but he was not taken seriously. After all, he was a 23-year old who had not finished college. He was finally financed by the Los Angeles Chinese Chamber of Commerce and given letters of introduction and instruction by a branch of the White Lotus Society (ancient Chinese society that had fomented revolution for centuries). Sailing for China in June of 1900, he was said to have told friends, quite eloquently, "I go to topple the Manchus from their ancient Dragon Throne."

Lea's book, <u>The Valor of Ignorance</u>, was published in 1909 and created quite a stir with its prophecy of national decay, and even more of a sensation in military and naval circles which would use it as their testament – not long after the author's death (November 1, 1912) – for a preventative war against Japan. Its credentials as a sober, highly professional essay in the developing field of geopolitics and a work of military strategy were attested in the introduction by General Chaffee: "We do not know of any work in military literature published in the United States more deserving the attention of men who study the history of the United States and the Science of War than this."

According to O'Connor, Lea's book "hammered at the theme that national 'virility' was all-important, citing Japan and Germany as examples. 'A few decades ago Japan was almost a myth and the German Empire only a geographical possibility. Today they are considered equal, and in many respects superior, in strength and greatness to the other powers of the world, and for no other reason than that they have not become to-heavy with industrialism …

ADDENDUM I

Should Germany on the one hand and Japan on the other continue to adhere rigorously to these laws, resisting the deteriorating influence of industrialism, feminism, and political quackery, they will, in due time, by the erosive action of these elements to other nations, divide the world between them.'"

O'Connor wrote, "He devoted the first half of his book to inveighing against what he called the 'decline in the military,' which he believed was fatal to a major power. In the second half, he took up the problem of fighting a war against the Japanese empire, which he believed was inevitable. Partly this was because of profound differences between the two nations, 'One nation is a militant paternalism ... the other an individualist emporium where aught that belongs to man is for sale.' Japan had attained a commanding position in Asia through her victory over China in 1895 and her crushing defeat of Russia, on land and sea, in 1905. Meanwhile, Great Britain had become preoccupied in maintaining a balance of power with Germany, and was no longer a significant factor in Asian strategy."

"Then Lea proceeded to map out the sequence of Japan's march to supremacy," O'Connor wrote. "She would seize the Philippines because that would end American and European dominance in the western Pacific; 'the channel of Balintang is the Rubicon of Japan.' She would also occupy Samoa to dominate the South Pacific from Pago Pago, and Alaska to maintain control the North Pacific.

The Japanese could easily invade the Philippines and defeat the American and Filipino defenders, he wrote, because it was 'no complex military problem.' With an accuracy that would encourage belief that the Japanese planners used Lea's book as a blueprint, he predicted that the Japanese would land at Lingayen Gulf and Polillo Bight; that the Americans would find Manila indefensible;

that the Japanese would capture Manila in three weeks (it took them twenty-six days, actually).

The Japanese, he said, would take the Philippines, Hawaii and ... then proceed to the invasion of the American West Coast."

O'Connor wrote that Valor was destined to be a handbook for a startling number of military and naval leaders throughout the world, including Field Marshal Lord Roberts and Kaiser Wilhelm, "But its most fervent readership was in Japan. There it sold forty thousand copies, went through twenty-four printings and was required reading for every army and navy officer. Something of a furor erupted when plans for its publication were announced by a Japanese firm in 1912 after the previous government had forbidden it. In Japan it was published under the title <u>The War Between Japan and America</u> and was falsely advertised as the work of an 'American staff officer.' Hoping to appeal to a general as well as a professional readership, the Japanese publisher proclaimed: 'More interesting than a novel, more mysterious than philosophy, this is really excellent reading matter for Oriental men with red blood in their veins.'"

The Papertrail
by Marvin Edwards – December 2, 1997
Fatal Vision

A young general could have prevented the disaster at Pearl Harbor – if anyone had bothered to listen.

On Dec. 7, 1941, the Japanese made a "surprise" deadly attack on Pearl Harbor. Actually, it should have come as no "surprise." Warnings that Japan was laying the foundation for such an attack were first made 32 years prior to the bombing.

ADDENDUM I

The alert was issued in 1909 in a book titled <u>The Valor of Ignorance</u> by a young American named Homer Lea. He was both partially blind and a hunchback. Lea attended Stanford University, and while there he developed a deep interest in the Far East, especially China and Japan.

Lea traveled extensively in China and assisted the Chinese during the Boxer Rebellion, serving as a military advisor. For his efforts, he was made a general in the Chinese army. He also was a supporter, friend and military adviser to Sun Yat-sen, the founder of modern China.

By invitation from Japanese military leaders, Lea was invited to Japan. They tried, but failed to convince him to join their growing armed forces, promising to give him a commission in the Japanese navy. Proud officials of the Japanese Naval Office even showed him a confidential map of Eastern Asia, which showed the entire region under Japanese control.

Lea wrote a second volume in 1911 called <u>The Day of the Saxon</u>. In it he predicted the decline of the British Empire, and a future attempt by Japan and Germany to divide the world between them.

The following are excerpts from these two publications:

"Silently, without haste, slowly, with an intentness which is conscious of neither hesitation nor diversion, this militant empire (Japan) moves across the sea. The nation vanishes. It has been metamorphosed into a soldier ... Japan draws near to her next war – a war with America – by which she expects to lay the true foundation of her greatness.

"In a war with Japan, there are other conditions of preparedness that will augment the rapidity of her conquest – (i.e.) the movement of her troops and naval forces to positions adjacent to the theatre of war prior to a formal declaration of hostilities."

Lea then discussed how the Japanese would take the Philippines. "The conquest of these islands will be less of a military undertaking than was the seizure of Cuba by the United States; for while Santiago de Cuba did not fall until nearly three months after the declaration of war, Manila will be forced to surrender in less than three weeks." (Japanese forces made their first landing on Luzon on December 10, 1941. They entered Manila on Jan. 2, 1942, 23 days later).

"The conquest of the Philippines is no complex military problem. Japan, by landing simultaneously one column at Dagupan (Lingayan Gulf) and another column of the same size at Polillo Bight (Lamon Bay), would strategically render the American position untenable. These points are equidistant from Manila." (A U.S. War Department study of the Japanese invasion of the Philippines released in November 1942 called "The subsequent landing of the two main invasion forces at Lingayen and at Lamon Bay ... one of the most brilliant moves of the entire war in the Far East").

Lea continued: "[The U.S.] and Japan are approaching, careless on the one hand and predetermined on the other, that point of contact which is war. Nothing can better serve the interests of Japan, or any nation under similar conditions, than the characteristic indifference of this Republic to the dangers threatening it."

ADDENDUM I

Lea's uncannily accurate prognostications were ignored or ridiculed by all but a handful of officials with both the War and State departments. Like Cassandra at Troy, his gloomy warnings were unheeded, and the disaster at Pearl Harbor was the price we paid. His books were read and praised by such figures as Germany's Kaiser Wilhelm, Russia's Lenin, and Britain's Lord Roberts. <u>The Valor of Ignorance</u> became required reading for all Japanese military officers. The book went through 24 printings in Japan under the title <u>The War Between Japan and America</u>. It also was a textbook at the Japanese War College, as was shown by their following Lea's strategy in their invasion of the Philippines and the strike at Pearl Harbor before a declaration of war.

One of the very few American military officials supporting Lea's analysis was former U.S. Army Chief of Staff Lt. Gen. Adna Chaffee. In fact, he wrote in the introduction to <u>The Valor of Ignorance</u> publication, stating: "We do not know of any work in military literature published in the United States more deserving the attention of men who study the history of the United States and the Science of War than this book."

One of Lea's important sources of information was his study of Japan's record of aggression against its neighbors. It makes erroneous the belief by some that we provoked the Japanese attack by boycotting essential goods needed for Japan's growing industrial complex.

As early as 1871, the Japanese strategists recognized that to make Japan supreme in the Pacific area, they had to occupy both territory on the Asian mainland and the numerous islands extending over thousands of miles in the

Pacific. Their first target was the Linchiu Islands, which were occupied that year.

In 1875 they occupied Russia's Kurile Islands to the north, and a year later they seized the Bonin Islands. Their first real military test came in 1874 when they attacked China without a declaration of war. That victory resulted in their annexing Formosa (now Taiwan) and the Ryuku Islands. This was followed by occupation of the Pescadore Islands.

Finally, it was time to go after big game. They set their sights on Russia's Liaotung Peninsula, which included Port Arthur. On the night of Feb. 8, 1904, Japanese torpedo boats made a surprise attack on the Russian Fleet based at Port Arthur, completely crippling the ships. Two days later, Japan declared war on Russia. The Russian Baltic fleet was then sent to engage the Japanese navy. Under Admiral Togo, the Japanese annihilated the balance of Russia's navy. With this victory, Japan seized the southern half of Sakhalin Island, and made Korea a protectorate, annexing it in 1910.

As he predicted, Japanese conquests continued after Lea's death in 1912. Germany owned hundreds of islands in the Pacific known as Micronesia. The three major chains were the Marshalls, Mariana and the Caroline's. Some of these islands bring bitter memories to our armed forces that served in the Pacific in the Second World War. They include Kwajalein, Palau, Eniwetok, Yap, Saipan and Truk. The First World War was started by Germany in 1914. Just one month after it began, Japan declared war on Germany, and immediately occupied all of their islands. They also seized Shantung Province in China, which had been controlled by Germany.

ADDENDUM I

In 1922, Japan became a signatory to the Washington Naval Disarmament agreement that limited both the size and number of capital naval ships. They then ignored the agreement, building battleships and carriers, and also fortifying the many islands they occupied.

Japan next decided to use China as a military practice ground for both its warriors and the new weapons they had developed. In 1931 they grabbed Manchuria. In 1933 it was Jehol. Then in 1937 they made a full scale attack against the heart of China. That struggle was still going on when they attacked Pearl Harbor, the Philippines, the Malay Peninsula and Singapore, as well as the Dutch East Indies. They felt Russia was no problem, because in the west they were reeling under attacks by the German military juggernaut.

Homer Lea received no recognition until the Japanese attack at Pearl Harbor. Yet, unlike the vague predictions of the 16th century astrologer Nostradamus, Lea's forecasts of future events were factual, very specific and amazingly accurate. The early successes of the Japanese proved that <u>The Valor of Ignorance</u> was more than just the title of a military text. Through our ignorance of the aggressive plans of both Japan and Germany, many millions of lives were lost. Lea saw the smoldering long before the flashpoint was reached.

Simply put, Lea's message was "eternal vigilance or eternal sleep."

The American Reader's Library published a reprint of <u>The Valor of Ignorance</u> by General Homer Lea (1909), from which I have taken the following quotes:

> In a war with Japan there are other conditions of preparedness that will augment the rapidity of her conquest – viz., the movement of her troops and naval forces to positions adjacent to the theatre of war prior to a formal declaration of hostilities.
>
> The popular belief that the United States is free of opportunities for invasion is all "tommy rot," if allowable to use an expression that we think more apt for our purpose than elegant in style. Briefly, and to the point – no nation offers more numerous opportunities for invasion by a foreign nation than does the United States whenever cause therefor is sufficiently great to induce preparations by any other nation that will beat aside our resistance on the sea.
>
> In the course of time no one knows when or how soon, the family of nations may get to playing at cards, and beyond the sea, perhaps will be found a "full hand" against our three "aces" – the Navy, Coast fortifications, and the Militia.
>
> Twenty years ago Japan recognized the inevitability of war for the suzerainty of the Pacific. It was this prescience that caused the Mikado five years later to voice solitarily his objections to the United States establishing dominion over the Hawaiian Islands.
>
> This Republic and Japan are approaching, careless on the one hand and predetermined on the other, that point of contact which is war.

ADDENDUM I

Nothing can better serve the interests of Japan, nor any other nation under similar conditions, than the present characteristic indifference of this Republic to dangers threatening it.

Japan is now supreme, in a military and naval sense, on the Asian coast north of Hong-Kong. China has been eliminated from these seas, as has Russia. And by Japan's alliance with Great Britain, the elimination of British power in the Pacific, as we will hereafter show, has been accomplished subtly; even with the smile of Buddha has this been done. There now remains but one power for Japan to put aside in order to make her supreme in the Pacific, with all which we have shown that term implies.

That nation is the United States.

The present strategic positions of Japan are, though relegated to the Asian coast, absolute in the command of those seas. By consulting the chart of the Pacific, it will be seen that Japan cannot strengthen her position nor lay foundation for future supremacy by war with any other country other than this Republic. The value the Pacific possessions of this nation bear to Japan is that they determine her possible supremacy of Pacific littoral. These territories consist of Alaska in the North Pacific, Hawaii in the Central, Samoa in the South, and the Philippines in the East.

The value of such a position is not due to its own productivity, but to the wealth of all the nations whose trade routes pass its turreted shores.

Nearly fifteen years ago the value of the Hawaiian Islands,

and the necessity of their possession to any nation who would be sovereign over the Pacific, was recognized by Japan. When this Republic annexed the islands at that time, Japan alone protested and notified the American Government that she would not then, nor at any time in the future, acquiesce in the control of the Hawaiian Islands by this nation.

The conquest of the Philippines is no complex military problem, but is, on the other hand, so simple and direct that a few words will make it apparent. The American forces defending these islands do not exceed fourteen thousand, plus five thousand native troops, all of whom are based on Manila. Japan, by landing simultaneously one column of twenty thousand men at Dagupan and another column of the same size at Polillo Bight, would, strategically, render the American position untenable. These points of debarkation are almost equidistant from Manila, and are connected with it by military roads, while a railroad also connects Dagupan with the capital.

The impossibility of defending Manila with the force now stationed on the islands is seen in the strategic advantages inherent in Japan's convergent attack. These two columns, more than double the strength of the American force, converge on Manila at right angles. Advancing at equal speed, they remain at all times equidistant from the American position. Should the American force advance to meet either column, the unattacked column, being as close to Manila as the American force, could throw itself in between. The Americans, separated from their base by an army equal to their own in strength, and facing a second army also as large, would be in a position wherein their

ADDENDUM I

capitulation could alone prevent their complete destruction.

If the American forces, on the other hand, should remain behind their lines at Manila, they would, in two weeks after the declaration of war, be surrounded by overwhelming numbers. The lines about Manila, as was demonstrated during the Spanish-American War, are incapable of prolonged defense. An aggressive enemy in control of the surrounding country can render them untenable in a short period of time.

The following quotes are taken from the American Reader's Library publication of Homer Lea's book, <u>The Day of the Saxon</u>:

The potential power of nations is, contrary to general opinion, of no consequence if the capacity to make use of it for the specific purpose of war is wanting. This potentiality of a nation is inclusive of its people to the same degree as it is of the iron ore in its mountains and other resources of which no use is made for the preparation or conduct of war. Because of this the vastest empires did not disturb the calculations of Alexander nor Mohammed nor Genghis Khan nor Napoleon. The wealth and population of the United States excite no fear in Japan, nor does the vastness of the British Empire cast any foreboding shadow across those routes of march over which Germanic armies expect, in due time, to make their way.

Germany, because of her vast initial power, and not Italy, would, subsequent to the overthrow of the British Empire, succeed to the control of the Mediterranean and all that which is now British in or upon its shores. Italy would then become no longer free to pursue even her present

circumscribed destiny, but would pass completely under Teutonic domination not only by land but by sea.

It can be considered as a maxim that in exact ratio as the Teutonic race increases in power and domination the Italian kingdom decreases proportionately in these two factors. Because it is paradoxical that Italian national security is inherent, not in the successes of its allies, but in their destruction, do we finally ascertain the fallacious and artificial character of this Dreibund, in so far as the future of Italy is concerned in the dissolution of the British Empire.

The spirit of Bismarck has departed only to diffuse itself into the genius of his race. While other nations must await the suitable adjustment of conditions to human genius, Germany waits only for the opportunity.

The British Empire, in its relationship to German expansion and the consequent dissolution of the British dominion, has not to deal with the German people, but only with conditions that determine Germanic expansion. The German nation waits only as Bismarck waited for conditions to shape themselves. So imbued is this race with his ideals that it can do without his genius. It has become Bismarckian. His heavy spirit has settled upon it. It wears his scowl. It has adopted his brutality, as it has his greatness. It has taken his criterion of truth, which is Germanic; his indifference to justice, which is savage; and his conception of a state, which is sublime.

This nation has forgotten God in its exaltation of the Germanic race.

ADDENDUM I

The amalgamation of Austria, the amalgamation of Italy were blows to British power; but when England permitted the amalgamation of the Germanic race it prepared the plans of its own sarcophagus.

Germanic amalgamation has heretofore omitted three spheres – Denmark, the Netherlands, and Austria – that are strategically, politically, and economically more important to its world greatness than are all its other subsidiary states. Not until these have passed into the Germanic confederation will the world become cognizant of Germanic power.

In the future it can be considered as an established principle that nations will more and more make war without previous notification, since modern facilities increase their ability to take their opponents by surprise and to strike the first blow as nearly as possible to their main base. That this is true is shown by the fact that the number of wars undertaken without any prior declaration of hostilities in the nineteenth century is greater than in the eighteenth. During the former century there are recorded forty-seven wars begun without any prior declaration, while in the nineteenth eighty wars were begun without any prior declaration.

ADDENDUM II

UN Articles – Carrier Courier
Published on February 23rd, 1946:
General Assembly Concludes London Session
Many Decisions Reached
Assembly Next Meets in New York, September 3
By F/O Marvin R. Edwards

The largest body, and one of the two most important organs (the other being the Security Council) of the United Nations Organization is the General Assembly. It is composed of representatives of all the 51 charter members of the UNO. No one state is permitted to have more than five delegates holding seats in the Assembly. Five alternate representatives, and as many advisors and experts as required are also permitted each delegation. Any nation that is admitted into the U NO will be extended the same privileges and rights of the present members.

Functions and Powers

The functions of the General Assembly as stated in the UNO Charter, Articles XI, and XIII are:

1. The General Assembly may consider the general principles of cooperation in the maintenance of international peace and security, including the principles governing disarmament and the regulation of armaments, and may make recommendations with regard to such principles to the Members or to the Security Council or to both.
2. The General Assembly may discuss any questions relating to the maintenance of international peace and

ADDENDUM II

security brought before it by any Member of the United Nations, or by the Security Council, or by a state which is not a Member of the United Nations in accordance with Article XXXV, paragraph 2*, and except as provided in Article XII**, may make recommendations with regard to any such questions to the state or states concerned or to the Security Council or both. Any such question on which action is necessary shall be referred to the Security Council by the General Assembly either before or after discussion.
3. The General Assembly may call attention of the security Council to situations which are likely to endanger international peace and security.

Other functions include the initiation of studies to promote international law, ... international cooperation in politics, in the economic, social, cultural, educational, and health fields, and in spreading human rights and freedoms to all peoples regardless of race, sex, language, or religion. ... created at the San Francisco Conference of the UNO held last spring. Included in the detailed report which the Commission made were certain sections concerned with the General Assembly.

The Preparatory Commission recommended that the first session of the General Assembly be divided into two parts. The first part was to be concerned primarily with organizational problems, and the second part would be mainly devoted to independent items on the agenda.

The first part of the first session of the General Assembly was concluded last week in London thirty-five days after it began. During this period many discussions were held,

some of which became very argumentative in character. The frankness which high-lighted the London conference has done much to instill confidence in the UNO. At the League of Nation's conventions, decisions were always postponed, and speeches were usually evasive.

The provisional agenda for the first part of the first session of the General Assembly as recommended by the Preparatory Commission was completely covered. In most of the cases where a majority decision was needed, one was reached. Others are still being ironed out by one of the committees or sub-committees created for that purpose. Some of the noteworthy accomplishments of the General Assembly in its recently concluded session were:

1. The selection of the president of the first session of the General Assembly. He is Foreign Minister of Belgium, Paul H. Spaak. His election was made in a closed ballot at the Assembly's first plenary meeting. He will continue to act as president at the second part of the first session which will be held in New York on September 3.
2. Election of the six non-permanent members of the Security Council. These are Australia, Brazil, Egypt, Mexico, Netherlands, and Poland.
3. The election of eighteen members of the Economic and Social Council. The states that carried the most votes are: Belgium, Canada, Chile, China, Columbia, Cuba, Czechoslovakia, France, Greece, India, Lebanon, Norway, Peru, Soviet Union, Ukrainian SSR, United Kingdom, United States of America, and Yugoslavia.
4. The appointment of the Secretary-General (upon his recommendation from the Security Council), Norway's Foreign Minister was appointed to this ...

ADDENDUM II

5. ... of the permanent headquarters of the United Nations. It was also decided to set up temporary headquarters in New York until such time as the permanent area is ready.
6. The decision was reached granting refugees the right to carry on political activity against the government from which they fled.
7. The election of the fifteen members of the International Court of Justice.

Voting and Procedure

Each member state is allowed one vote. On all important questions a two-thirds majority of the members present is required. Considered in this category are "recommendations with respect to the maintenance of international peace and security, the election of non-permanent members of the Security Council, the election of members of the Economic and Social Council" and of the trusteeship Council, "the admission of new members to the United nations, the suspension of the rights and privileges of membership, the expulsion of members, questions relating to the operation of the trusteeship system, and budgetary questions" ... All other questions can be decided by a majority of the members present.

If a member state's financial contributions to the Organization falls in arrears to an amount equal to, or greater than that due from it for the preceding two full years, it loses its vote in the General Assembly. If the other members of the Assembly feel that the debtor state is in arrears through no fault of its own, it may still be granted the right to vote.

The General Assembly must meet at least once a year

in a regular annual session, and in any special sessions if necessary. "Special sessions shall be convoked by the Secretary-General at the request of the Security Council or of a majority of the members of the United Nations."

(The Security Council, its powers and function will be discussed next week.)

*ARTICLE XXXV, paragraph 2
2. A state which is not a member of the United Nations may bring to the attention of the security Council or of the General Assembly any dispute to which it is a party, if it accepts in advance, for the purposes of the dispute, the obligations of pacific settlement provided in the present charter.

** ARICLE XII, paragraph 1
1. While the Security Council is exercising in respect of any dispute or situation the functions assigned to it in the present charter the General Assembly shall not make any recommendation with regard to that dispute or situation unless the Security Council so requests.

The above article was followed in the Carrier Courier by one written in March of 1946 titled:

Security Council is UNO's Board of Directors
First New York Meeting Scheduled for Tomorrow
by F/O Marvin R. Edwards
(This is the fourth of a series of articles concerned with the historical background, recent progress, and future trends of the United Nations Organization).

ADDENDUM II

The key pillar in the United Nations Organization is the Security Council. Its members have the responsibility of making decisions that will have a bearing on the lives of all of today's generation and their posterity. There is so much that can be written about this body that it is imperative to devote two separate articles to this organ. This, the first of the two, will be devoted to the Security Council's composition, general functions and powers and method of voting.

Composition of Council

Eleven states comprise the membership of the Security Council. The five states holding permanent seats are China, France, the USSR, the United Kingdom and the United States. Six non-permanent members were elected by the General Assembly in January. They are Australia, Brazil, Egypt, Mexico and Poland. In the future, all non-permanent members are elected for two year terms, but the Charter specifies that three of the Nations gaining seats at the first election shall only remain for one year. A retiring member is not eligible for immediate reelection. Only one delegate is permitted from each member of the Security Council.

Functions and Powers

"1. In order to ensure prompt and effective action by the United Nations, its members confer ... responsibility for the maintenance of international peace and security, and agree that in carrying out its duties under this responsibility the Security Council acts on their behalf. 2. In discharging these duties the Security Council shall act in accordance with the purposes and principles of the United Nations.

3. The Security Council shall submit annual and, when necessary, special reports to the General Assembly for its consideration. 4. The members of the United Nations agree to accept and carry out the decisions of the Security Council. 5. In order to promote the establishment and maintenance of international peace and security ... the Security Council shall be responsible for formulating, with the assistance of the Military Staff Committee, plans to be submitted to the members of the United Nations for the establishment of a system for the regulation of armaments."

Voting Procedure

Just as in the General Assembly, each member of the Security Council has only one vote. All decisions on procedural matters must have an affirmative vote of seven members. One of the most delicate points in the whole charter concerns the voting method on all matters other than those of a procedural nature. In these cases, not only must there be an affirmative vote by seven of the eleven members, but all the permanent members must cast concurring votes. This is the rule which many authorities feel might become a source of embarrassment to the stability of the UNO. Nothing is mentioned in the Carrier about what course will be pursued when a permanent member not only fails to agree to the unanimous decision, but refuses to abide by it. Disagreements on the Council thus far have been amicably settled. It is hoped that such will always be the case. The future peace of the world hinges on it being so.